T0340025

Creating Brand Cool

In this intriguing blend of branding how-to and business memoir, an industry pioneer presents the thought process and tools to create a successful Ecommerce business by developing a distinct emotional attraction to a brand, beyond individual product offerings.

Leveraging her 26 years of experience in online marketing and branding, Joan Abraham reveals the thought process behind successfully addressing today's marketing challenge: clearly defining the business's brand essence using its owned social media channels to personalize the full character of the brand. *Creating Brand Cool* addresses the importance of developing a unique state of being that personally resonates with today's consumer. Abraham energizes the creative and strategic thinking for attracting and maintaining brand loyalty when the competition is a click away.

Appealing to branding and social media marketing professionals, as well as students in these fields, this book is a primer for building an online community and distinguishing a brand from the competition. It is relevant to all types of business, from small businesses to globally recognized brands.

Joan Abraham's focus on the Internet over the last 26 years has created new merchandising and marketing paradigms for branding in a global marketplace. Among her accomplishments are two one-hour specials for the *Oprah Winfrey Show*, the establishment of a network of video walls in shopping malls nationwide for advertisers, and online media campaigns for The Chrysler Corporation, NBC, ABC-TV, Phillips Van Heusen and the city of Detroit.

She currently heads up StyleBranding, Inc. which she founded in 1996. The company specializes in the next generation of online content for branding and marketing in the Ecommerce arena. She has recently retired after 25 at Parsons School of Design in New York where she taught Ecommerce Marketing and Fashion Branding Abraham developed the Ecommerce marketing course for Parsons in 1996 and graduated with a B.A. from the University of Michigan.

Creating Brand Cool

Brand Distinction in the
Online Marketplace

Joan Abraham

Routledge
Taylor & Francis Group

NEW YORK AND LONDON

First published 2021
by Routledge
605 Third Avenue, New York, NY 10158

and by Routledge
2 Park Square, Milton Park, Abingdon, Oxon, OX14 4RN

Routledge is an imprint of the Taylor & Francis Group, an informa business

Library of Congress Cataloging-in-Publication Data
Names: Abraham, Joan, author.
Title: Creating brand cool : brand distinction in the online
marketplace / Joan Abraham.
Description: New York, NY : Routledge, 2021. | Includes
bibliographical references and index.
Identifiers: LCCN 2020053026 (print) |
LCCN 2020053027 (ebook)
Subjects: LCSH: Branding (Marketing) | Internet
marketing. | Electronic commerce.
Classification: LCC HF5415.1255 .A274 2021 (print) |
LCC HF5415.1255 (ebook) | DDC 658.8/27—dc23
LC record available at https://lccn.loc.gov/2020053026
LC ebook record available at https://lccn.loc.
gov/2020053027

ISBN: 978-0-367-69315-2 (hbk)
ISBN: 978-0-367-69314-5 (pbk)
ISBN: 978-1-003-14134-1 (ebk)

Typeset in Sabon
by codeMantra

To Ken

Contents

Acknowledgements

This book is a labor of love devoted to a subject I am passionate about. I wouldn't be able to have the vision I have on the subject without my Parsons students who have always opened up the future for me. The caliber of work presented over the years has consistently kept my perspective ahead of the curve. Their professionalism and creativity have been my fuel. Isabella Taylor is the student we all dream of, an incredible prodigy talent who always makes me look so good, thus responsible for the cover illustration. My very special thanks to Heana Song and Nicole Dillon, ex-students and dear friends, who are my fashion Sherpas.

My good friends Bill Cella and Ira Carlin opened up a lot of doors to the advertising industry. They saw the vision I had and gave me great visibility behind the curtain. Dennis Swanson must be mentioned, whom I met at WLS-TV in Chicago. We both moved on to New York, he with ABC, NBC and FOX. He always offered me television programming time which encouraged me to keep up the pursuit. Bruce Block, a very talented dear friend, always fuels my creative thoughts with the ability to produce many of the innovative program concepts I have developed. Lynn Pregont was my partner in arms when she sold my fashion expertise to WLS-TV. Her marketing and media savvy made the video wall at the Trade Center a reality.

I have a special debt of gratitude to my friend Janet Rodgers whose support in getting through the book helped make it happen. I am most grateful to Janet for settling me into New York as I galloped on the scene in 1987, immersing me in New York style through all the right places and just the right way. By the way, Janet is the "consummate shopper" in Chapter 12. And lastly I must include Celia Sherred who always supported the work and the ideas as a dear friend who has nothing to do with the fashion or advertising industry.

Introduction

The ability to purchase a product through the computer and have it delivered directly to one's door was just beginning to impact our lives around 1994. The actual moment I realized the profound impact digital retail would have on traditional retail was during the holiday season in 1995. I could avoid crowds, the lines to check out, and carrying around my purchased gifts with the simple touch of a computer key from home. I knew then, there was no turning back. It took the retail industry a little longer to fully invest in the capabilities of the Internet to produce the most revenue-generating channel for the brand.

In the Dark Ages of 1994, there were no smartphones, or laptops and Google had not yet discovered the answer to just about everything. Jeff Bezos had just launched Amazon and the product selection was focused exclusively on books. He was surely a visionary for selecting an easy product with which to test the power of the Internet. Selling books could be accomplished without concern about fit or color.

Jeff Bezos also realized if the customer couldn't examine the product in person, the retailer has to make it as easy as possible to return the product. This "no risk" service encouraged the consumer to return and try again. Customer service was his number one focus from the very beginning.

Bezos' primary interest was getting the functionality of the process right as opposed to being focused on the profits for the shareholders. He concentrated on making the system work and making the customer happy. Not many CEOs overlook the grumblings from the board of directors about not distributing the profits among shareholders. For years he was losing money and he insisted on investing any profits back into the business, constantly learning about how best to serve his customers most efficiently. Knowing what Amazon has become today I think there is a message in its business model.

Back in 1995 who could even imagine selling shoes online, as the fit and feel are so critical? But Tony Hsieh, founder of Zappos, figured it out. Like Bezos, he realized that if you make it easy enough for the customer to try it and return it, the customer will buy even shoes online. Having thousands of different pairs of shoes presented right in one's own home is truly nirvana for many women. The convenience and impulse factors are too enticing. Like the traditional retailer Nordstrom, these companies adhered to the baseline principle; the customer is ALWAYS right.

In 1996, as a marketing instructor at the Parsons School of Design's newly established Fashion Marketing department, I was granted the ability to teach a course specifically on my new-found focus: marketing online retail. This led to the development of the course I still teach today, originally called "Ecommerce Marketing" now aptly titled "Social Commerce".

In my virtual classrooms, I share the insight and strategic knowledge with my global student body, who are able to interpret the language of the Internet so naturally, and together we have been able to create branding paradigms for the online environment that are unique and effective. Sharing strategic thinking with the students' online social skills gives all of us a look at where Ecommerce and lifestyle marketing are going. The students' intelligence, creative point of view and global representation have offered me as valuable a learning experience as the branding theories and practices I've passed on to my students. In sharing my story, it is possible to see how to creatively brand and develop online marketing strategies which can apply to a one-man shop or a multinational corporation.

My exposure to Ecommerce marketing has been through the eyes of traditional fashion branding and translating these branding techniques to the world of digital retail. Many examples stated in the book are personal experiences as I watched the online phenomena develop from its earliest stages.

It's been a fascinating ride to see the retail industry which exploded through rapid store growth and mall development during the postwar era finally shift its focus to the power and ease of the Internet. With the Internet being such a prevalent fixture in all of our lives, I am eager to share my most valuable experiences and my vision of what Ecommerce will become. This book is about the merging of retail, advertising and entertainment to create excitement in the marketplace of the Internet.

Chapter 1

Anyone Can Be
an Amazon.com

The good news about the Internet is that everyone has a voice. Anyone can be seen and heard. The bad news is that this creates a lot of noise.

A website should be informative, or clever, controversial or unique; and a combination of all the above is even better. If you have a product that no one else is offering you have a great advantage online with a global audience. You can be found through Google even if you are headquartered in Iceland. Since most of us offer goods or services that are readily available in the marketplace, the challenge becomes how to attract the consumer to your website.

Branding is defining a sense of difference and then being able to communicate this distinctiveness. The process of branding creates an awareness and emotional recognition for the product. Great branding creates a strong desire for the product or service. What makes Nike "*Nike*"? Or, what gives Influencers their allure? Each represents a certain something you and I crave.

Recognizing the sheer abundance of almost everything, it is easy to see why creating a noticeable presence is essential in a world that is virtual. The branding process is the *seduction of the sell*. How do we elicit that must-have *feeling* in a product or a service?

Why is the Internet the most valuable point of brand contact? For most of us, our daily habits and lifestyle patterns require digital interaction all day long. We are truly a global community when it comes to the web. We already shop globally as easily as we shop locally. No matter the size of the business, a brand's website must communicate and transact clearly and easily, or it will be very tough to compete in this global bazaar as time goes on.

A brand's website is its face to the world. In the online world, branding is about using today's technology and creatively engaging the consumer in the *experience* offered by the brand. Today retail is all about the experience. The fragrance brands are expert at this approach when using television around the holidays. Think about the Dior fragrance commercial at Christmas time where Jennifer Lawrence sweeps us into her fantasy world, and we are to become the idealized Jennifer simply by using the fragrance.

Very soon technology will be used by brands to create this complete surround-sound sense of fantasy through virtual reality. If we can engage our customer with something beyond our core merchandise offering, something related to her desires then we have positively tapped into his/her psyche. The Internet allows us to take the consumer on a journey through information, experience or engagement. The more complex our culture becomes, the more fantasy we seem to enjoy. Retail has always been about understanding how to create an environment that makes the consumer forget about day-to-day reality and escape in some form to a more pleasant "daydream".

Social Media Allows a More Personal Brand Experience

Retail has always been about the experience. The Internet gives us a whole new set of tools to work with. We are at the very beginning of stretching our imaginations in all new ways to create these yet unknown experiences. Until social media became a massive merchandising/selling tool, the website environment looked pretty much like a catalog.

Using social media to communicate with the consumer brings out the *personality of the brand*: "Who are you really?" The word "Who" is meant to emphasize how the brand is humanized through its unique qualities: its ability to relate to its audience. Take a look at the Citibank website: specifically the Life and Money section. This is a bank that features a complete section on its website dedicated to informing its clients and visitors how to upgrade their *lifestyles*: how to navigate through all the aspirational goals one has as a young adult. The site features sophisticated choices when it comes to travel, health and wellness, and what cultural highlights are available, unusual museums, wine tasting, restaurants and thought leaders along with what's *hot* at the moment. This is the experience that Citibank provides as a part of their brand culture. Citibank as a financial institution is establishing its sense of *cool* with the places it *partners* with: those brands offered up as goals for its audience to aspire to. Selecting specific brand partners, such as places to travel, determines the client profile Citibank is talking to. The more sophisticated the partners are, the *cooler* the brand is.

The ultimate goal is to make the brand so magnetic that the consumer craves the product or service as part of her self-identification: "I love how I feel in my Cole Hahn shoes carrying my Coach bag." "Citibank helps me articulate and fulfill my long-term lifestyle goals". These brands make us feel good about ourselves and how we present ourselves to the world. The consumer is reacting to the brand essence, which is way more powerful than just the product.

The explosion of social media, this powerful new selling/communication tool, is a game-changer. Social media is as vital to the retail branding process as it is essential for all sectors of the economy that interact with the public.

Social Media Exposes the Brand Character

Social media is uniquely a two-way communication vehicle, whereas traditional advertising is one-way communication telling us what to do. The more personal the brand voice in the social channels, the tighter the relationship with the consumer. The social channels communicate the heart of the brand.

These communication tentacles work most effectively when they enhance the brand personality. The social channels, also known as *owned media*, give the brand the opportunity to develop a more personal interaction with the user, adding depth to the brand experience. Owned media refers to communication channels that the brand itself owns and controls.

The consumer can communicate more *casually* through the social channels. Social communication is considered more of a brand *soft sell*. I often refer to the social channels as the suburban branches of the brand's flagship website when speaking about ecommerce and online retail.

The branding strategy of any company needs to incorporate daily social media communication into the overall strategic plan. If one is selling a product or service online, one must be engaged in social media regularly. After so many years of trying to reach as many people as possible with one message, even the largest retailers are capitalizing on the personal engagement social media offers.

This is not how we are used to selling products and obviously it is easier to talk about than to execute—especially for a small operation. But no matter how big or small, every brand will benefit exponentially by using all of the social channels to promote and sell products.

The more you use your owned social channels for merchandising and engaging, the more you increase your audience. More people have access to your online presence than any other avenue of exposure; therefore, one's social channels need to constantly reinforce the same feeling, message and experience that the brand has created through its store, promotions and media expenditures. All of this online visibility must be part of the overall marketing strategy.

The idea of a company's social channels representing the character of the brand is only going to intensify. For the up and coming consumers, Millennials, Gen Z and forward, daily fresh content has come to be expected. You own these communication channels and each channel is capable of enhancing the brand image and selling merchandise. Now it is imperative that you use these channels to do exactly that.

Creating fresh, interesting, entertaining and informative content everyday was not part of building a business only ten years ago. Today it is vital and a great place to showcase your individuality. Competing today means focusing on how to define yourself as a business and exposing your uniqueness in the market.

The more content you create that has value, the more popular you are. The fresher the content circulated through the owned social channels, the quicker the rise in visibility through Google rankings.

Communication through the owned media channels substantially supports online visibility and recognition. Being able to define exactly what gives your product its *character* is the number one goal in the world of Ecommerce. This is where the branding process begins. This is the brand distinction.

Through the Internet I can now live in Des Moines and have access to Chanel, Gucci, any movie ever translated to DVD, or, literally anything I have read about or seen as long as it's online. This is totally now! This was never possible before. The level of sophistication among the general public is as viable in Des Moines as it is in Chicago because we now have local-to-global news in real time capturing our attention all day long.

The Value of Ecommerce to Niche Markets

The impact of Ecommerce on niche markets, the luxury market for example, highlights the value of a global audience reach on the bottom line. It was once believed that selling luxury goods online diluted the exclusivity of the brand. The luxury market brands were very slow to actually offer online transactions. The fear was the elimination of essential personal service, and the dilution of exclusive appeal of their products.

The luxury market brands are quickly learning that to compete they must offer sales through the website. If you can afford a Gucci bag you are part of the exclusive group that can own a Gucci bag. Exclusivity inherent in luxury merchandise comes from the ability to afford the merchandise. Luxury goods companies are working hard to offer exclusive service capabilities. Services like online personal shopping by appointment or same day delivery of merchandise are services that combine the best of in-store and online shopping. During this highly unusual time when the public is reacting to a pandemic, the brand's services are quickly becoming more noticeable in grabbing the consumers' attention.

As younger generations continue to replace Baby Boomers who traditionally shop in stores, the web will more emphatically be the primary source of information and consumerism.

The social action of shopping in a store **will always** serve that purpose in our culture. Town centers will never die out. But the **need** to go to the physical store is greatly diminished by the ease of Ecommerce. The Spring of 2020 has changed everything. The bloated market of shopping centers is going to slim down considerably. Shopping Centers will be offering experiences only available on-site: eating, movies, amusements and augmented reality. Digital shopping and browsing is going to be the norm.

Throughout the book we will focus on specific branding elements that reflect the brand personality or character. They are introduced in this chapter and mentioned throughout. These branding elements are all interconnected and describe the creative process used to define what a brand represents. This book will give the reader the direction needed to use creativity and innovation in building brand recognition.

Customer Service Is the Center Core of the Brand

The websites of the mid-to-late 1990s had to offer services that would make it easy for the consumer to **engage** in the Brand's online presence. If you couldn't try the merchandise on or see it in person, the vendor had to make it very convenient to shop and return.

Jeff Bezos realized early on that his knowledge of how to create an infrastructure, a technology platform focused on cutting-edge customer service and ease of use, was the gospel online. He also realized that he could enable many brands the opportunity to sell through his platform. In return Amazon would be paid a small percentage of the sales. Since most retail brands were completely unfamiliar with the Internet and treated it as a foreign language they had not yet learned, they were happy to have Jeff Bezos handle the back-end infrastructure of getting the products to the customer. This was especially vital to getting retailers involved with Ecommerce back in the 1990s. Traditional retailers were afraid if they didn't have a state-of-the-art presence operationally it would hurt the brand.

The Value of Online Advertising for Brand Awareness

On the Internet the education, information, engagement and sales can take place with each view or exposure of the product. This has changed the way brands are advertised. No other point of purchase or media is that powerful.

New media has become much more targeted and efficient for today's marketing principles. In times past it was all about reaching the broadest audiences possible. Advertisers targeting the mass market could afford television and needed to be on television to keep their engine going, constantly increasing market share. With social media we can pinpoint whom we send our message to. And the online tools for communicating have a lower cost of entry than traditional media like television, newspaper and magazine advertising.

More importantly, with new media you are not advertising to people who do not relate to your product, so there is very little wasted expense. Using advertising budgets in the online environment is a more direct method of reaching out to your specific audience. Online advertising buys can start with very low expenditures which increase the audience substantially. Learning how to use search marketing, keywords, and communicating in the social channels is a valuable branding asset which we will go into in more depth throughout the book.

You can advertise online with a budget of any size to be in the game. To demonstrate the selling power of the online environment, a brand's website sales increase upward of 20% consistently year after year since the early years of 2000. To compare, the average increase in yearly store sales generally hover around 1%–3% per store per year.

Naturally as sales increased so did the online advertising budgets. Over the last five years online advertising has been eating into the budgets for more traditional media at a rapid pace. If executed properly, online marketing can consistently increase online sales and it will precisely measure who is responding to your messaging, affording the brand more precise customer data.

When I started developing online content back in 1995, the online departments of any major company were generally located in the basement with a minimal budget just so the company could say they were in the game. Those budgets have gradually grown into the billions, in large part because of the preciseness of online advertising.

Today, building a brand is about *personalizing* the brand or the **image** of the brand in the minds of the consumer. Being able to pinpoint the message becomes more meaningful especially for products that have niche audiences. For big broad-based brands, they too have to learn how to speak to segmented audiences. And the more personalized the voice, the better.

Like everything else, the idea is to keep reinforcing the brand message creatively and emotionally until it registers in the consumer's mind, and then you keep going continuously. The Internet offers up all new tools for messaging and all advertisers need to adjust their messaging to capitalize on the value of these digital capabilities.

Advertising is also beneficial for lending credibility to an otherwise unknown product. If you go to a website that has resonated with you through advertising, you are more willing to trust the brand and online buying process. There was no brand *Wayfair* a couple of years ago.

Think about whether you would trust them if their commercials creating awareness didn't help lend credibility to the brand.

The online only brands, or **natively digital** brands like Wayfair.com that have substantial budgets to advertise on television, have the ability to create valuable awareness and credibility quickly because of the reach and frequency of the messaging. Wayfair is everywhere. Their commercials are constant on television especially during the holiday season. And if you purchase a Wayfair product, Wayfair follows you around the web for a very long time with suggestions related to your purchase. This is called **retargeting** and is a very effective way to connect with a consumer, although it can be annoying. It has to be effective because it is ubiquitous and I am constantly retargeted with suggestions connected to my last purchase, or serving up a product I left in a shopping cart.

Wayfair offers *free shipping on everything* including large household items. That's a very powerful draw. They also offer low "direct to consumer" prices. During the pandemic when the public is in isolation, their homes have become their castles. Wayfair commercials are constant. And just like the shoes from Zappos, if the shipping is free and the returns easy, WHY NOT? Wayfair's follow through and exceptional customer service all aid in pushing the consumer to the actual transaction. Would I recommend them? Absolutely!

Understanding the value of an Ecommerce site and new media advertising allows smaller companies communication access targeting exactly who they want to reach. And it allows big merchants to become more personal.

The Value of Strategic Partnerships for Branding

Fashion and Music are the magic elixirs that can bring a sense of *cool* to a product. Most fashion brands have very limited marketing budgets. If the fashion brand's **style quotient** *makes a statement*, teaming up with major lifestyle advertisers can create new merchandising/marketing tools to bring awareness to both partners. Like all partnerships the brands have to be serving the same audiences.

Fashion and music partners add a sense of cool to a brand with big advertising budgets looking for that distinction: the sense of *being in the know*. Matched with the appropriate fashion brand, any lifestyle product can take on a sense of *cool* with a fashion brand partnership. This also creates exposure to new audiences within each of their target markets. The fashion brand can always use the exposure. These brand relationships are very engaging in creating a lifestyle feeling about the brand.

As we lay out these major marketing themes that help us build distinctiveness, we will continue to explore how these marketing trends work in today's marketplace. Defining the brand and the world the product lives in is the starting point. Customer service, strategic partnerships, cause marketing, entertainment and online communication are key strategies that help give the brand exposure in our overabundant market. The message here is to figure out how to make your brand relevant to your audience using all these new tools we now have available.

Remember, the good news is anyone can open a stall and have the world as an audience in our global bazaar. Getting the attention of the consumer to react to our product is the challenge: how to create real excitement around the brand through entertainment and information.

Chapter 2

The Website as Brand Central

Now that the retail industry is fully aware of the impact of Ecommerce and social media, the role of the website and the use of social media marketing have exploded throughout the industry. With good reason digital retail or online shopping allows us to indulge in all the things that make shopping fun: we can send the outfit to our friends to see what they think; with a few keystrokes we can check to find the lowest price; we can get the opinion of many others who have tried the product; we can see if the product runs true to size.

The link directly to your selling space can be placed in so many different locations. It's no surprise that so many millions of dollars are shifting to the Internet when a simple link can take you directly to the website and the point of purchase.

The website needs to be thought of as *Brand Central*. You have a global audience, so you better have your game face on.

The power of the web is not going to diminish. If you are not aggressively tending to your website and social channels, you will not stay competitive. Once we can visualize this global bazaar where anyone anywhere can offer something for sale, we can see just how competitive the playing field is, hence the importance of selling through uniqueness.

Let me begin explaining the process of branding by defining what a brand actually is. It is more than just the product: it's what makes me give up my lunch money for months for that Supreme jacket, or those Nike Flyknits.

A brand is a **promise**. It is a promise that it will deliver a value in the best, most efficient way and will always do so (Hameide 2011, p. 8).

Branding is the emotional element that is embedded in the product; I call it the *soul* of the product. Branding is showcasing the character, or the personality of the product. That's why social media is so valuable a communication tool. Social media offers the opportunity to show off what makes you special; to constantly reinforce your *cool*.

Where the Branding Process Begins

Once a product is ready for market, it is necessary to carefully and thoughtfully pen all of the descriptives that fully represent what the product and the company stand for. The branding process starts with answering the question; what characteristics are imbued in the product? Addressing each one of the following descriptives taken from *Fashion Branding Unraveled* (Hameide 2007, p. 6) gives definition to your greater purpose as a business owner.

Entity
Distinctive Features
Idea
Promise of Value
Return
Equity
Relevance
Identity
Positioning
Innovation
Consistency
Image

Each one of these qualities needs to be defined very granularly, and then etched into the minds of everyone working for the brand. This positioning needs to be a part of everyone's thinking; not just the marketing department, but the entire company needs to understand how to represent the brand in completing daily tasks. Everyone is a brand ambassador today and it starts with all those working for the company.

The Art and Science of Branding

The *Art [of branding]* is about balancing creativity with consistency to endow a brand with an emotional appeal that builds on its heritage. This includes the evolution of the brand with changing cultural trends...The *science* [of branding] is in measuring a brand's strengths and weaknesses across the entire purchase funnel (Perry and Spillecke 2013, p. 6). Perry and Spillecke go on to say, "the *promise*, the consistency of the promise and the ability to stay relevant creatively and emotionally."

Now let us examine why it is so important for the website to represent *the brand* as precisely as possible.

The Ecommerce location is a brand's most central location, available for everyone universally. Creating a stylized presence on the website is essential. Shopify.com is a website offering 360-degree support for anyone who wants to start a business on the web. This website will put any entrepreneur in business today with all of the parts and professionalism needed.

There are websites that make it very easy to build a website describing service businesses very effectively. Companies like Wix offer the infrastructure templates for websites. All you need to do is fill in the blanks with the images, copy and the functionality needed on the site. These websites are very efficient and used by companies big and small. Just make sure that every detail of the site represents how you **feel** about your product. It's that *emotion* you need to translate to your consumers. I suggest investing in a graphic designer to help you lay out your site unless you are one. That *Trust* factor again.

You can also spend very large budgets on special effects and creative visual style like Nike, a brand that has always been on the cutting edge digitally. There are losers and winners in all price categories. What you need to keep in mind is you compete by defining your uniqueness, and you get noticed by selling through that uniqueness. Understanding how to articulate a brand's uniqueness in its merchandising and its marketing is a key component to keeping the brand desirable.

Corso Como is a shopping development in the South Street Seaport area of Manhattan. The concept and developer are imported from Europe. The website is so whimsical and fresh looking. It's not as formal looking as most fashion/retail websites yet the look is so distinctive and sophisticated at the same time. No matter how big or small your brand, it is imperative to understand and define a brand's reason for being or the competition will always stunt your growth.

The Experience Offered on the Website

The website can no longer be a static presentation of the product without much of an *experience*. If you find exactly the product you're looking for when visiting a site, that's effective online selling and the basics in site development. But our job as retailers is to seduce the customer, create the fantasy that takes her out of reality for a moment. Even in a difficult economic climate, there are a lot of products competing for the consuming public's discretionary dollars.

Buying a product is creating the escape into the person we *want* to be.

One of the basic functions of the website is to motivate sales. The website should be an experience that motivates the customer to check out that one little thing not really needed but it would be fun to have. You want the consumer to come and "hang out" on your social channels. You want the consumer to position your brand as part of his/her *identity*. Your brand goal is to be the customer's Style Sherpa in multiple areas of her life activities. As the seller, we need to create that experience for the shopper.

What is the brand experience? This is where lifestyle merchandising becomes very important to the shopping experience. We grab the consumer's attention by relating significantly to her desires and lifestyle needs. We will focus on lifestyle merchandising in detail throughout the book.

Lifestyle Marketing

We have to think about how to create events and interest through the website as well as how we merchandise the website to draw in the customer and have her engage with the brand regularly. Notice I speak about visiting the brand regularly. Daily engagement is expected from preferred brands of the younger set. This is where social media communication enters the picture. A brand's daily emails are a good start for getting the customer to visit the website.

Technology in the Retail Environment: Omnichannel Retailing

In the last couple of years, the emphasis has been on bringing technology into the purchase experience. You can find something online and purchase it in the store, or just pick it up at the store for immediate gratification. One can find a product in the catalog and purchase it in the store. All of the selling channels are being organized into one system, which is something new and very difficult to achieve from an operational perspective.

The old management system for retailers with different selling channels was that each distribution channel, i.e. storefront, catalog, website, functioned as a separate business. Now retailers have to streamline all of the points of distribution so the consumer can shop however it's most convenient. This is customer-centric operations, as opposed to each one of these channels being separate businesses of the retail brand.

Now it's all about customer service. If you don't harmonize your system, your competitor already has. It makes the shopping experience much more serviceable to the consumer. This process of allowing the customer to purchase from any channel and pick up and return from any channel is called **omnichannel retailing**. Most stores have converted to this business model because their competitors were doing it and now it is essential.

Technology is being brought into the store in many ways these days. This is all part of the brand experience, and the blending of in-store and digital retail is going to be more and more noticeable.

A great example of the value of omnichannel retail is Walmart's Halloween commercial from 2019 showing kids picking out their favorite costumes online, and then having them available and ready for pick up by Mother curbside at the store. No disappointment of running out of the coveted costumes while making sure they were received in time for the big night. That is seamless, multi-channel retailing geared to the customer's needs.

Aspiration Is *Cool*

When marketing online you have to create or define the *character* of the brand. Whether the brand is JCPenney or Prada you should always create the feeling of aspiration. The more sophisticated, hip or well designed a product looks, the more desirable it becomes. And you can make anything look and feel good. It's all about knowing your customer and relating to her level of aspiration. You never want to talk down to your consumer.

The above statement is one of the most important in communicating a marketing message. The more you respect the consumer with sophistication and intelligence the more she will want the brand as part of her identity. That is unless you are appealing to young guys. Apparently, they love to look dumb. You want the consumer to think, "that's who I want to be!" not "why would I ever want that?" The more aspirational you are in your presentation, the greater the audience relating to your brand.

Don't forget that you always have to deliver on the brand promise. You'll lose a lot of ground very quickly if something happens to question the brand quality. Examples of major and minor brands having to deal with public relations disasters pop up all the time. It's how you handle the disaster that affects the brand. Take the case of Toyota, having the reputation of a very safe, affordable car, and then a couple of years ago experiencing a number of recalls: one being about the brake pedals that were getting stuck under the floor mats on some of the models. It was a disaster for a brand known for its dependability.

All of a sudden Toyota's brand was tarnished not only by the defect, but their very delayed reaction to this serious safety hazard. Only after a great deal of complaints from angry and frightened consumers, did Toyota accept the problem and address it. It was so timely for the American auto industry because American cars were finally winning back a long-lost reputation of being considered safe and dependable.

This is a very important lesson to remember. Brands need to be cared for and groomed as if they are a living entity. Problems need to be addressed instantly and with compassion to maintain the brand image.

Social media is the voice of the public responding to today's brands. If a company responds and continues to communicate with its constituency during a crisis, people will continue to trust the brand. Social media can be used to read the audience and respond very quickly to problems affecting public perception. Don't forget this lesson. As long as the public has a voice through social media, the brand has to be transparent and honest, ALWAYS.

Cause Marketing Is *Cool*

It is fascinating the number of lifestyle brands that have responded to the civil rights issues of *Black Lives Matter* and voting in the 2020 presidential elections. This demonstrates how companies can speak to something they truly believe in. This kind of cause marketing as I discuss later in the book can impact our culture in a good way. And if you do it right and significantly embrace the cause, that's *cool*.

You can create brand recognition by the pricing of a product. Or, you create brand quality by the communication of what you stand for as a brand, and the ability to attract people to that feeling. Apple's iPod is a leader in creating desire around a brand that everyone wants to identify with. Apple is a brand that every age group is interested in. Three major issues attract the consumer's attention: a site has a product that no one else has, it has the best price for what you're looking for, or, because the personal experience and comfort level draws you in every time.

Ecommerce and Brand Recognition

The retail game has changed so much with Ecommerce that traditional retail brands are now competing with media companies. The lifestyle magazines, *influencers* before the time of online *Influencers*, are now getting into the retail business through Ecommerce. Media companies are creating new revenue streams using the power of their brand recognition to sell products: NBC, ABC, FOX, Vogue, *Gentleman's Quarterly*, Town & Country, Gourmet, Oprah. They are using the likeability and trust they have established through entertainment and information to create an additional revenue stream.

Taking advantage of this brand awareness and trust, builds "brand extensions" valuable to the corporate entity. To be able to buy the outfit that Kerry Washington is wearing in her hit television series *Scandal* is pure ecstasy for millions of television viewers. Talk about the *Sizzle of the Sell*...the entertainment value is built right in when the networks start retailing the wardrobes from their original drama and comedy series programming.

Diane Ellis, then CEO of The Limited, was smart enough to partner with ABC and the program *Scandal* starring Kerry Washington as the main character Olivia Pope. The Limited developed a capsule collection modeled after Olivia Pope's wardrobe, and then built a promotion around the collection tied to the TV show as part of The Limited's campaign targeting working women. Kerry Washington's empowering character Olivia also helped the *attitude* The Limited was selling. The campaign was a great success for The Limited as the collection sold out, and it substantially reinforced the brand character among working women.

And Then There Is Everyone Else

Along with non-retail brands getting into the retail business online are thousands and thousands of people with good ideas. You don't even need to have your own site to sell merchandise. You can go on eBay or etsy, or simply set up a Facebook page, and the world can find you. This means that major retailers are selling a click away from Susie Smith who is selling hand-made sweaters from her living room, a small distinctive product, that thanks to Google search is selling more than she ever dreamed possible to people all over the globe.

Brand Awareness Provides Trust

ShopNBC.com is no different than any other online general merchandiser with a no-frills approach. Even though the website is very basic in its presentation people trust buying their Cuisinart Food Processor at ShopNBC because it is the combination of two known brands.

For instance, would you buy a Cuisinart from a site called brandslimited.com or Macy's? You know the Macy's brand is trustworthy. Macy's has to stand behind the brand promise. If you charge a purchase like a Cuisinart on the Macy's website, you know you are going to get an authentic product and it is going to arrive in a timely fashion and you can return it if you change your mind. If you don't know anything about brandslimited.com, and your friends have never heard of it, you don't trust that site as much as you trust Macys.com.

Brand recognition and familiarity also give the consumer a sense of security and trust; the product can be purchased with a credit card and the product is going to arrive and be returnable if it's not right. Seeing the brand name over and over again makes the brand familiar and builds the trust that name recognition affords.

Search: Keyword Marketing

SEARCH is the magic weapon for an online presence. **Search marketing** is all about knowing the proper keywords to identify with your site: key words are how you define your brand, your products or services in the marketplace. A consumer types a phrase or question into Google related to what she is looking for. If any of the phrases she inputs matches the keywords in your brand/business description, your site listing will come up in the search. You can buy keywords, meaning allocate ad dollars to keywords to get your brand higher up in the search results. Common words are more expensive than specific phrases. Active social channels also move your brand up on the search list. Google loves active brands. This puts more importance on daily social media comments.

Search is more like a science and it is invaluable because it allows anyone to find you no matter how remote your location is. The more specific a keyword, the more targeted the search. Even as a small local merchant you have to create trust, especially online. You can create online advertising that can appear just in your market area, or you can pinpoint certain zip codes and saturate those areas with brand awareness through promotions, advertising, signage and philanthropy. These are all tools for creating awareness and trust.

Search is essential to being in business on the Internet.

Search marketing is critical because it allows the smallest local merchant to have a presence all over the world via Google. It's all about letting people find the site online. Search marketing is an essential *first step* in an awareness campaign for any brand big or small. Search *keywords* are the most essential if you want to be found on the web.

Search is about using the right **keywords** in designing and registering the site. Keywords are the words that you use to describe your online business. Use all of the keywords that relate to your products. You can use phrases too that are more directional for the consumer. Multiple keywords together are called *long tailed* keywords. For instance, instead of just *watches* you can use *luxury watches* or better yet *Rolex watches*. Keywords are the map to your website. The book *The Long Tail* (Anderson 2006) spends a lot of time talking about how search advertising has leveled the commerce playing field because keywords and search advertising allow anyone no matter how small or how remote, to be seen and accessed. *The Long Tail* describes this phenomenon as *Selling Less of More*. Through the web Google keywords effectively guide anyone searching for your product or service right to your front door no matter where you are.

Using Google ADwords with your defined keywords is tedious and precise. But if you get in the rhythm of addressing every promotion with the content mapping and defining the keywords, this procedure guarantees profits and increased engagement. You are planning and strategizing into the social media system.

Content Mapping

There is a valuable process called *content mapping* which involves mapping out the main objectives of the campaign and then planning the communication online checking the content against the objectives. This allows the core brand values to be emphasized properly. The core of your content centers around the target market, your media partners and your goals.

Once you have mapped out the main objectives of the campaign and how the core values fit into those objectives, you have a "universe" for the merchandise presentation and subject matter for your daily content for the campaign. You take each circle and address it in a social post with a link to the merchandise. Using the keywords that you develop for each circle, you have the adword advertising and the content pages, or landing pages, that link to the keywords. This becomes your content calendar and when mapped out ahead of time it allows you to carefully layer personality and brand characteristics into the brand strategy.

The Value of Design in Creating the Brand Experience

Design is another *cool* factor. Everything is more desirable when a design element is factored into the value of the product. Think Apple and the meaning of this statement vibrates.

Target has taken design to the masses in the most dramatic fashion and built a brand image around its positioning statement, *Design for Less*. A well-designed product is more attractive and makes the user feel better about ownership. The following examples demonstrate how design affects the product value and how the consumer feels about the product.

Target has put an aspirational element on its brand by focusing on style and design. It began with its quirky marketing and advertising campaigns, which are truly distinctive in the world of retail advertising. The phrase *Design for Less*, the Target *promise*, coupled with that always recognizable logo of the red and white target, create enduring brand identifiers.

This sense of style was reinforced with Target's strategy of hiring recognized product and fashion designers to design products specifically for Target beginning with the introduction of Michael Graves. Michael Graves, a high-profile architect, was asked to design products for everyday kitchen products to be sold exclusively at Target. This was a number of years ago and quite revolutionary at the time. How clever of Target to use a high-profile designer from another industry to set a design image for a mass merchant retailer.

Target's communication puts the excitement into everyday products as generic as Tide and Clorox through their commercials. Target's relationships with high-end designers from around the world give the brand style credibility. And that style element filters down to all the products that are part of the brand... including Tide.

Target speaks up to its consumer community in the partnerships it creates, the merchandise that it develops, how it presents the merchandise, and how it educates Target consumers about the design provenance, or why the designers they partner with are so well-known. When Target started selling products designed by Isaac Mizrahi, it was before Isaac's television show or much national exposure outside the fashion industry. By choosing Isaac as a partner when they did, he was considered cutting edge, one who could make a difference in the direction of fashion. This gives the brand substantial street cred among the fashion trend setters, but Target had to educate its audience on why Mizrahi's designs were *cool*. Target put Isaac on a cross-country bus with his garments and educated women across America's heartland as to just who Isaac Mizrahi is and why he lends design value to the Target brand. When the Target customer wears her Isaac Mizrahi pea coat with extra pride and self-confidence, it's because she understands the significance of the design and the designer.

To stay one step ahead of the crowd, Target is constantly bringing in new cutting-edge designers with exclusive capsule, or limited, collections, to keep its fashion image truly fashion driven. And each capsule collection sells out immediately in most cases.

Target's partnership with Missoni, which crossed over a number of product categories, was nothing short of fabulous. If you didn't know the name Missoni, or what the design statement of Missoni is, you sure have an idea after seeing the marketing materials Target created for the launch. The promotional videos developed back in 2011 clearly demonstrated the Missoni brand style and the merchandise flew out of the store before normal people (non-fashionistas) had a chance to know about it.

We don't think of just saving money at Target. We want to identify with the sense of *cool* that Target has created. We want Target to help us define who we are. The extra cache of style puts Target right at the top of the list of exciting brands to be a part of because it's cool and available to so many people on so many economic levels. Target educates and trains the consumer's eye to enjoy the style nuances that add value to our perception of the product.

Another example of the value of design is described in an article from the *New York Times* business section May 17, 2007 titled "Design Helps HP Profit More on PCs (Darlin 2007)" reporting how

> Hewlett Packard's effort to transform its personal computers from low-margin commodities into more stylish devices has started to pay off. As shown by the company's fiscal second-quarter earnings ... a new PC strategy has become a major driver of growth ... Furthermore, H.P. is also making more money on each PC it sells.

No *frills* means *no thrills* and in a world of abundance there is not much of a market for the mundane.

Just as the mass merchants realized that style and design sell more product, online retail needs to commit more attention to the presentation of the merchandise and creating that "must have" thrill.

I talk a lot about the automotive industry because the industry is built around the differentiation of style, and because I'm from Detroit. The automotive industry has streamlined their businesses to be competitive in a global market. In the auto industry marketing an *attitude* is as important as the price and performance of the car. Design has resurfaced significantly with American cars as the field of competitors has grown globally.

To further show how design can affect the value of a product, an automobile is brought to life wrapped in a coat of style. Surely the "swoon" of style can add value to the feel of the car.

Ben Stein put it this way in an article for the *New York Times* on the American Auto industry. In the article dated May 27, 2007, yet still very relevant to this discussion, entitled *The Dream That Once Was Detroit (Stein 2007, para. 11)* he states,

> in America, you are what you drive...A car is what you aspire to, what you dream of, who you want to be. A car is a bigger, better, badder you.... The Cars of the Fabulous '50s {there is a book with that name; look at it and be amazed at what Detroit used to make} and the early 1960s were gorgeous, powerful, lush... The American product, Detroit iron, was the stuff of which dreams were made.... Then it all fell apart. Starting in the late 1960s (except for the Corvette, always the design leader in North America), American cars became shapeless blobs. The problem is that management stopped making cars that Americans wanted to buy and drive. The Japanese and German models, even if made in Kentucky, just look, drive and feel better, offer more of a thrill and are more reliable than what Ford and G.M. and Chrysler generally turned out. But look what happens when Detroit offers a model that consumers want, like the Chrysler 300C or the wholly redesigned Cadillac STS-V. The dealers can barely keep them in stock.

There's that *thrill factor* again. Just look at the words that Ben Stein uses to describe how a car can make you feel: "the stuff of which dreams were made."

In 2020, as the American auto industry regains its stature in the American market, it is delivering cars that are considered world-class, design driven and performance ready. And I can say that all these years later Detroit is delivering on the promise and they are very competitive in this country once again. The right fashion brands can increase the *swoon* factor of American automobiles.

The sense of style has to be pronounced in every detail of the product and the messaging, down to the smallest element. Style emotionally affects the broadest spectrum of consumers. *Style* is a level of distinctiveness that goes with *anything*. It speaks up to an audience. It declares a sense of perception and intelligence. That's why Apple and Target have such a broad appeal. Both brands speak intelligently to the audience, make everybody feel good and the interaction makes our everyday life better.

Graphic Presentation Personalizes the Product

Getting graphic on the product doesn't discriminate by price; any product can handle the scrutiny. This enhances the presentation of the product and gives the consumer additional information since she can't *touch or feel* the product. Online it is essential to show the details.

Presenting a graphic visual of the product in the storytelling is magnetic online. Only allowing glimpses of the products in the video storytelling so popular today with the luxury brands, doesn't translate powerfully online. It makes it difficult for the viewer to become *engaged* in the garment.

Style and Design Enhanced with Partnerships

Style is about individualism. It is about making a statement, standing out in a crowd. In order to create a sense of style one must have a full understanding of the object to which style is applied; whether it's a product identity or a personal identity. *Style is about using your eyes to get others to use their eyes.* Whatever you are trying to promote, or feature in a crowded environment, attention to detail is imperative.

To be successful at creating personal style, one must put one's whole self into expressing who you are. This applies to products as well as individuals. It's a highly disciplined act but very rewarding. It's about reinforcing your assets and intelligence by presenting these traits as the first thing someone notices about you.

Personal style reflects how you feel about yourself. If you are aware of what it is that makes you who you are, then you can create personal style with your presence. The same applies with product branding. The brand image is centered around the product distinction and uniqueness. One must understand what it is that makes the product valuable in the marketplace because that is the distinction on which the brand image is established.

The online environment allows us to go way beyond the product itself in developing a sense of style. We can build a whole world associated with our product to communicate what the brand stands for. The general idea is to make sure that as a team, representing the brand from different departments or disciplines, all the pieces that make the finished product must fit into the brand mold. As the web environment continues to populate with Ecommerce opportunities, it becomes more and more important for the brand to look and feel unique.

Design, style and *animating the product* online are essential, and global in appeal. Design and style are magnetic in the ability to cause a response from the customer.

The ultimate goal of any brand is to have the consumer desire the brand for self-identification: i.e. Nike in the 'hood, or Rolex in the luxury market, or Apple, among creative types.

The Internet is not a catalog. There are so many digital tools to facilitate customer relationships and bolster the animation or attention of the product presentation on the Internet. In a traditional store, it's about the windows that lure us through the front door, the merchandise presentation, traffic flow and most importantly, the customer service. These key design elements need to be translated to the web with different tools: digital tools that can create that enticement.

The Consumer Loves Stories

When presenting products, it's a good idea to tell a story about the items. It gives the products dimension. A company that does this very well is dsoder.com. The site sells scented candles. There are many different scents on the site with the strangest combination of flowers, herbs and spices. Jeff Newsom, the owner of the brand, tells the story of what inspired him for each scent. These funny, quirky stories explain how the fragrance and name came to be and give the candles a personality. His stories also create very clever VidBits or short video stories for daily social communication. https://vimeo.com/403352409.

The Website as Flagship

Getting back to the idea of the website serving as *Brand Central*, a website should reflect the full range of a brand's products or services. A fashion brand can fully immerse us in the brand experience through the website by offering the complete assortment of the brand's products. If a brand's website only offers a small selection, or a fraction of what the brand offers in-store, it is frustrating to the online shopper. The website as *Brand Central* should feature the merchandise the way a flagship location would be merchandised.

It is now 2020 and just in the last six years or so, have the big European luxury brands offered Ecommerce websites. These brands would present beautifully produced websites, but nothing was for sale. The European fashion sites were much more visually seductive than their American counterparts, but you couldn't buy anything.

This is probably why the website Net-A-Porter, one of the premier online luxury retailers, has the recognition and awareness it has today. Natalie Massenet had the vision to realize that a transactional luxury retail site available to a world-wide luxury audience seemed like a winning concept; and it has been. Net-A-Porter is now the leading digital retail brand for luxury products. This company is really responsible for getting luxury brands to see the value of selling merchandise online.

This chapter has introduced the major elements for developing the website as *Brand Central*. As we continue dissecting the branding process we will see how customer service, strategic partnerships and lifestyle marketing, take on so many dimensions and serve as the major themes for creating Brand distinction in the global marketplace known as the Internet.

References

Anderson, C., 2006. *The long tail*, 1st ed. New York: Hyperion.

Darlin, D., 2007. Design helps HP profit more on computers. *New York Times*. May 17.

Hameide, K., 2011. *Fashion branding unraveled*, 1st ed. New York: Fairchild.

Perry, J. and Spillecke, D., 2013. *Retail marketing and branding: a definitive guide to maximizing ROI*, 1st ed. Hoboken, NJ: John Wiley & Sons.

Stein, B., 2007. The dream that once was Detroit. *New York Times*. May 27.

Chapter 3

Putting the Sensory Appeal into the Sell

Consistency Is Key for Brand Distinction

When we talk about communication this includes everything that comes from the brand. And I use the word *everything* to be as all-inclusive as possible. Everything from the brand that is introduced to the public must reinforce what the brand wants the public to *feel*. As mentioned, this is even more important inside the company doors. Those who work for the brand are brand ambassadors and everyone needs to understand and transmit the consistent feeling the brand represents.

Defining exactly what the brand stands for determines everything that is communicated from the brand. That list of brand descriptives I mentioned in the last chapter is the bible for everything developed to promote the brand. Online promotional events need to represent the "lifestyle" of the brand character. When a brand develops a lifestyle to identify with, it gives the brand dimension. This goes beyond just presenting merchandise; it enhances the *emotional* appeal of the brand.

The Necessity of Tailoring the Brand Voice

The audience you are trying to attract determines the tone and voice of the content you create, and the means of distribution. An example: hip-hop music videos sent around the web will attract a younger audience. Using the elements of music, storyline and visuals this format can be very effective for reaching this group. Changing the music to jazz and the characters and language to speak to Baby Boomers will give you more relevance to that over 75 audience using the same music video format. The more accurately you incorporate the voice and tone of your audience, the more successful the response to the message.

How Do We Get the Message to Our Audience?

Thirty years ago, the media sources were very controlled: a limited number of magazines, three network television stations, billboards, radio and local newspapers. It was very easy for brands to control the message.

One of the clearest examples demonstrating the radical erosion of traditional media sources is cable television, which slowly started to infiltrate the domination of three (eventually four including FoxTV) broadcast networks. Cable brought on an explosion of targeted networks with a very specific focus on clearly defined audiences: the Golf Channel, National Geographic or B.E.T.

The next new media to come on the scene was place-based advertising, or local promotions: point of purchase promotions. As an example, shopping centers now run advertisements in their main court areas, and this is considered "place based" advertising. Malls then became another area where national advertisers could advertise locally.

Our company, ADmotion, was actually one of the first to capitalize on offering national advertisers an alternative use of their television commercials on video walls placed in shopping centers nationwide: www.stylebranding.com/admotion.

Now advertising exists wherever there are eyeballs, including video monitors in elevators, on the workout equipment at the local gym, and at your gas pump. Wherever there is public traffic there is advertising.

How do we decide where to advertise and how to get the message out? I use the phrase **surround sound media** by which I mean reaching your consumer by putting messages wherever your consumers are. The plethora of places to put our messaging is daunting to say the least, but the data we have available makes it more efficient to *surround* your audience with your messaging.

The more personal the media, the phone for instance, the more relevant the message has to be. The logic is to be very mindful when speaking to your audience. Once an individual is turned off by the brand with inappropriate messaging it is very hard to win them back.

Technology has had such an impact on the media landscape and the proliferation of media resources has become overwhelming; no one is able to keep up with all of the choices available. Today the available data provides more dimensional lifestyle or psychographic elements giving media buying another dimension that must be determined beyond basic demographic decisions.

Brand Symbols

The Target Stores' red and white bullseye is one of the most effective brand symbols right up there with the Nike swoosh, the Apple, and Macy's fervent effort to brand the Macy's Star. As soon as you see the symbol, you know the product. My mind immediately goes to Target whenever or wherever I see a red bullseye that Target so craftily claimed in the early 80s. The response to how the consumer *feels* when she sees that symbol, hears your music or sees the brand name registers the impact of your branding effort.

A brand is *a living thing*. It's designed to elicit an emotional response and if it is not examined and analyzed constantly with regard to how the public is responding to the brand essence, it will fade into the distance quickly.

For small companies with virtually no media budgets, social media becomes even more important for branding. The brand owns its social channels, and these channels provide endless space in which to translate the brand message daily. Just keep in mind that the messaging has to be informational, interesting or entertaining for engagement.

Emails

I am a firm believer in the ability of email to keep the customer engaged in your brand. In most cases our audience has an edited email inbox delivering information and opportunities from desired or preferred sources. Emails are direct access from the brand to the consumer. At the very least, even if the email is deleted the brand name flashes by the consumer's conscience as it is being deleted. And, if the email recipient has a moment of time when the email appears, she will click on the link to check things out. That's when you get the sale. If emails weren't effective selling tools, I wouldn't be getting the flurry of daily emails from my selected brands multiple times a day.

Featuring individual items or events in an email, allows the recipient to focus on the message or product highlighted. Mentioning too many elements in one email doesn't grab the attention of the recipient.

Email supports all your marketing efforts and even by itself can be a mighty weapon in servicing your customers. It is a *proactive* message that goes right into your customer's email box.

The Internet has reach beyond anything we have known previously. The limitless space this channel offers reminds us of how we need to address this landscape. The Internet is the "Rome" that all roads lead to and you better spread the word on how to get there.

The role of all other media now must focus on directing the consumer to the website: the point of purchase, the point of information and the point of engagement. If you let the world know how to access the brand, they will come. This is true for all products and services.

Retail marketing means promoting all selling channels; store, catalog, website; but the focus has to psychologically drive the consumer to the website as *Brand Central*.

Personal Means Respect the Recipient

We are in a time of monumental change because of technology and the instant speed of information flow. Today's media landscape is pervasive and invasive. Therefore, we must be more sensitive and thoughtful about how we approach our messaging, where we place it and the data we accumulate. If we are fully mindful of the information we have access to, we must use it thoughtfully to best serve our customer.

We will get a broader response if we ask only for information that can help serve the customer better. You don't need to know a person's income range to promote to them through email. You need to know their lifestyle so you can address their needs more efficiently.

The message will be absorbed if we are sensitive to customers' privacy. If marketers are aggressive, overbearing in their approach, they will not get the information they need, and they will not be well received in this give and take relationship. Your brand image depends on *how* the data and information is acquired and used.

Both mass media and social media have a valuable role in today's communication landscape. But given a choice and budget constraints, personalized media delivers a great deal of interaction for the money spent.

The biggest news about social media is that it is engaging; it requires a response from the viewer. Since social media requires the viewer to take action, we know right off that he or she is interested enough to respond.

So many marketers are having a field day, albeit nervously, with this new world of interactivity and broadband technology. Customer conceived commercials, audience selected naming contests and texting to vote for the contestants of *Dancing With the Stars* or *America's Got Talent* have changed how we think of media and entertainment. It is impressive how television programming has taken on the interactive connection of the Internet.

Anything goes as long as it fits into a carefully planned strategy for building a brand. New, fresh ideas are the fuel for future growth. The highly visual nature of fashion lends a lot of seduction to the product presentation. Make the product the "star" of the show or in this case, the message.

Online Lifestyle Networks

Online advertising is also about finding the online sites related to your consumers' lifestyle. If your budget affords online advertising on lifestyle sites the first question is what sites are your targeted consumers visiting? It's always good in planning a banner ad campaign to test smaller, more select sites for banners to see the response you get. You will have many more *qualified* visitors see the message, the more specific the website is to your target customer.

You can go on iVillage to reach women, or ESPN to reach men, and those websites will deliver a lot of "eyeballs" just like network television. You can also buy smaller networks of sites that relate to specific lifestyle categories.

Bundled Lifestyle Networks

Now that there are so many websites relating to so many different audiences, there are online media companies that offer media buys consisting of *networks of lifestyle sites*. These companies are in the business of accruing large numbers of lifestyle websites that are bundled to create a "specialized" network for an advertising buy. These media companies offer the brand a specific audience whether it's fashion sites, sports sites, hip-hop sites or medical sites. These media services can offer localized, regional or nationwide recipients.

These companies also monitor the activity on these media placements *daily* and consistently reconfigure the buys moving the banners to the sites that draw the most traffic or response. This is very targeted and effective. Monitoring the site daily and moving the message to the sites that are most productive is called **optimizing** the media buy.

You can spend any amount of money on these buys. If you only have $1,000, you can buy a banner ad campaign with a small geographic radius. The online media company guarantees so many click-thrus for your advertising buy. A **click-thru** is when the viewer clicks on the banner ad to get to your website. It usually costs about $1.60 for each click-thru with these online buys, which means 625 click-thrus will cost $1,000.

If it takes a month to deliver the number of click-thrus you were guaranteed for $1,000 then your ad runs for a month. If it takes two weeks for 625 people to click-thru to the site from the ad, then the ad only stays up for two weeks. If all of your click-thrus are used up quickly that's good news so you shouldn't be disappointed. You only pay for what is delivered. Once you have 625 click-thrus, the ad comes down. You can make these buys, locally, regionally and nationally.

Mobile Advertising Is All About Getting Personal Responsibly

Mobile advertising is going to explode going forward. Every advertiser knows that in today's world everyone always has a phone with them at all times. Mobile advertising with Apps and direct links to the website, is the next area of focus and marketing growth. The phone requires *the most thought* in selecting the appropriate messaging because it is the most personal.

The more we learn about our customers the better we can accommodate their lifestyle issues. If properly executed, the more personal the
message, the more responsive the audience. This is not the end of mass
media. It is using mass media personally.

The Value of Media and the Research
We Have Access To

Today the sum of all media blended together can be measured very
precisely. So not only do you need to decide *how* and *where;* you need
to think about *what* data you are looking for on every promotion you
execute. This is the strategy development.

Online marketing is all about capturing specified data and how that
information is used to make the next message even better.

Understanding what is possible in measuring ad words and keywords
opens up all kinds of opportunities for learning more and more about
our consumer. Using this information for planning the brand strategy
is valuable knowledge for any company. The analytical world of social
media marketing will positively grow any business from a Mom & Pop
operation to major corporations. The most forward brands are capitalizing on all this information. Social media marketing has certainly
gained a tremendous amount of respect in today's marketing spectrum
as reflected in the ad dollars spent online these days.

Serious amounts of money are flowing from traditional advertising
into online advertising because online delivers real time information
about the consumer, and, it's where the audience is these days. Businesses are getting very sophisticated in understanding and using online
media buying very precisely.

When buying traditional media such as the television networks, the
magazines, websites, radio, etc., these media companies will provide
mountains of data on how the public uses their communication channels. But the day-to-day information that a company receives from its
owned media is very valuable for learning how to define your distinction
or brand character.

Lifestyle Marketing Is All About Getting Personal

Media selection is directly related to lifestyle choices; how the customer
uses his/her time and where we get our information. Media choices are
so diverse today, creative thinking plays a big part in media selection.
Because we have so much contact directly with the consumer, empathy
should be a part of every decision. And empathy comes with experience.
Every marketer needs to ask, "How do I really understand the everyday
needs of my consumer, ... and be ready to address those needs on the

spot?" This is the secret of marketing today. We all know that the deeper you can tap into a consumer's emotions, the more attached the consumer becomes and the more trust is developed.

The emotion comes from trust and trust comes from knowledge. We have the ability to talk to our customer even though she may be half-way around the world. The interactivity available allows us not only to track our consumers' behaviors, but to inquire and measure their personal needs, desires, and goals in life.

Lifestyle marketing kicks into high gear when a brand starts to fully engage in using its website for personalization. The idea of personalizing the brand exercises all new creative communication muscles.

Offering information beyond the brand's merchandise selection helps build relationships with your consumers. Promotions related to *lifestyle* create *communities* around the brand image. This reinforces the sense of understanding and trust and loyalty. The brand becomes a source for lifestyle information.

Lifestyle partnerships among brands expand the reach beyond the brand's core audience. It also provides worthwhile content for daily brand communication. Building on brand partnerships with media companies can offer additional promotional opportunities. Advertising today is about getting personal with the consumer and the traditional media companies have overhauled their business models with their owned online media channels to be able to personalize the message for their advertisers. The next chapter is a broad overview of different media opportunities available today to help a brand create the sense of creating *Surround Sound Messaging*.

Failure Is a Part of Success

It is essential to understand that no one has all the right answers, and failure is an important part of succeeding in this economy. The *New York Times* ran a fascinating story in the magazine section a while back entitled "What if the Secret of Success is Failure? (Tough 2011)" In this environment of technology evolving faster than anyone can keep up, you need to use your head and your heart and go for it.

If you are forced to be afraid of failure for fear of losing your job, you are in a work environment that can't keep up with modern technology and online marketing. Social media campaigns must be thought of as ongoing, constantly new, and requiring DAILY care and pruning. Quick and on-going decisions need to be made related to the daily responses to your brand message. The campaign strategizes need to be outlined and scheduled thoughtfully and thoroughly in advance for daily content, and then executed while daily refining the results. This is the key to understanding social media. Everything in the online environment is moving at a rapid pace and you can't belabor "perfection". That's not what the online environment is about. It's about always fresh, always moving and authentic.

The lesson is to continue to refine the things that work and test new things all the time. Remember the online environment is *always a work in progress*.

When I moved back to Detroit from New York in 2008, working with Maggie Allesee, one of Detroit's major philanthropists, we developed an online campaign to improve the image of Detroit. We sent weekly emails that told a video story about individuals who were passionate about the city. The stories were about individuals from all ends of the spectrum: all who represent and have influenced Detroit's distinctive culture: www. detroitpocketsofcool.com.

We had the freedom with social media to make the videos any length. I personally was infatuated with each individual we interviewed and had a hard time editing the stories, but we learned very quickly that when sending email videos the stories have to be very short to be opened. The first VidBits (short video stories) we sent out were too long. If the stories were kept to 30 seconds to two minutes, more people opened the videos. Today I say keep the video messaging down to 15–30 seconds and no longer than a minute. Enhanced content can always be available on the website for those more interested in the subject.

Keep trying new things. It will make you more expansive in your thinking. You may catch hell for the mistakes, but you'll get over that and you're a much more effective creative. Today's messaging is renewed daily, not weekly or monthly like a magazine. Mistakes can be repaired instantly and you keep going. The goal is to not make mistakes but it does happen to the best of us. Just look at the *New York Times* and the daily listing of apologies for mistakes in print.

The Return on Investment with Social Media Is Engagement

The ROI with social media is *customer engagement and interaction*; not just eyeballs and visibility. Make sure you understand this distinction. Engaging the audience in the brand experience is critical today, and you are going to see that planning social media content can create a give and take between the consumer and the brand that is suited to the consumer's lifestyle. This is as valuable to the brand as a sale because when the customer responds, it shows a desire to belong to your *brand community*.

The advertising industry no longer has full control of the brand perception. Now it is being molded and influenced by the public at large. This is a critical recognition in understanding online marketing. The technology and bringing the consumer into the brand building process is successful online branding. Everything online can be precisely measured related to the dollars spent: who engaged with the message, and how much product was sold. Both the engagement and selling factors are invaluable today.

The customer now has an integral role to play in shaping the brand essence. Social media only has value if you allow the honest flow of communication to take place. If a brand reacts quickly and prudently to negative comments on social media then the market will trust the brand. It's been difficult for many big brands that have had complete control of the brand image to let go of that control. The goal is to set the tone and put it out there everyday, and evolve with what the market feeds back to us.

This book does not elaborate on the science of online media buying, but being aware of how these tools are used is critical for selling exposure. There are many places to find information more specifically related to the tactics of online media, starting with Google which can take you inside this world related to search engine optimization: keywords, search, ad words and how to build a campaign understanding the use of these elements. Google today has a multitude of tools for measuring their advertisers' presence online.

Hootsuite is a website offering extensive information on creating an online presence through search and social media advertising. Understanding these formulas is extremely profitable for any brand from Susie Smith, remember her, who started in her living room, along with Nike or Nordstrom.

As marketers, it is critical to be as articulate as possible in communicating exactly what your brand stands for and how you are communicating that to the public. This prevents confusion from the customer and doesn't blur the essence of the brand. Since interactivity with the brand is constant and ongoing, the brand identity and image need to be crystal-clear anywhere there is a brand touch point.

Reference

Tough, P., 2011. What if failure is the secret of success. *New York Times*, 14 September.

Chapter 4

Research Is Your Sherpa

Research is the foundation for all marketing decisions. Like many in the retail business I used to think marketing decisions were *gut* decisions. I *knew* those people. Now we have so much information at our fingertips, we have to take advantage of what can be learned about our consumers so that we are able to stay completely relevant. It is also necessary to be selective and very focused in how we access and use the data.

Let me share some basic information that will help guide you through the research process. This information comes from *Retail Marketing and Branding: A Definitive Guide to Maximizing ROi* (Perry and Spillecke 2003). The following is a checklist of how to approach the process of research.

Research Process

- What kinds of data are needed?
- From whom do we get the data?
- When is it accessible or conveniently obtained?
- How should it be recorded, collected, stored?
- Why is it needed?
- Adhering to the above will help keep the project focused.

Methodologies: Qualitative; Quantitative; Primary vs. Secondary Data

Qualitative data approximates or characterizes, but does not measure attributes, characteristics, or properties of a subject or "phenomenon". It is not based on precise measurement and mathematical claims. Fashion analysis is often qualitative, as fashion phenomena cannot be "counted".

Quantitative data expresses a certain quantity, amount or range. Usually, there are measurement units associated with the data.

Primary vs. Secondary Data:
Primary data is collected from first-hand sources, using methodology such as surveys, interviews, or experiments, for a specific research purpose. Secondary data is already collected and available from other sources. Secondary data sources include censuses, information collected by government departments, organizational records and data that was originally collected for other research purposes.

Research Methods:

- Surveys
- Workshops and focus groups
- Employees
- Social intelligence/social listening

Evaluating Internet Sources:

- Whose website is it?
- Is it reputable?
- Is the material dated or when was it last updated?
- Is it primary source material or secondary presented?
- Can information be corroborated?
- A complete reference to cited material given

I include the above information as a general guideline to the data gathering process. Data is critical for steering you through the campaign as to where your audience is and how they are responding to your messaging. It also provides the rationale for your positioning. Data plays a more important role than ever as we learn more about our customers and the ability to serve them personally. As I mention throughout the book, being responsible and respectful with the data is key to customer trust and loyalty. Use it thoughtfully.

Reference

Perrey, J. and Spillecke, D., 2013. *A definitive guide to maximizing ROi*, 1st ed. Hoboken, NJ: John Wiley & Sons.

Chapter 5

Surround Sound Media for Online Branding

Cloud Living and the Impact of Data

As most of us are aware, Google has spent billions of dollars to build huge data centers, or 'server farms' around the world, enabling it to store enormous quantities of personal data. As the world of online advertising spreads like wildfire, information is now more than ever the foundation of communication. The information and messaging we receive daily has been getting more and more refined, driven completely by the data.

All of the information is accessible by clicking on a link and the content is downloaded to us. The storage of data through the server farms frees up the storage space in our computers. In our world of *cloud living* there is so much information available to us, it is necessary today to select what information we want coming to us. We sign up for emails we are interested in and based on those emails we are also sent email ads from related companies that specifically appeal to us because of the habits we exhibit during our daily routine. Wherever we go on the web we leave crumbs called *cookies* that can follow our visits. A company can track our visits and feed us advertising relating to the goods and services we visit. This is called **retargeting**. If you search for Sony electronics you will then get a message from Panasonic following the logic that you are looking for electronics products.

Because our research capabilities are getting more refined in learning about our consumer, the methods of communication delivery are also getting more refined and targeted. That means we will be paying more attention to the ads we get because they are more in tune with our personal needs.

Research Directs the Media Efforts

With so many choices in the marketplace, the job of marketers is to determine which media channels reach the customer best during her daily routines. Today's research analytics can slice and dice demographic information to give us an overwhelming amount of data related to the group we are spending our marketing dollars on. Customer segments can be refined into more granular groups either by race, gender, age, geographic locations and lifestyle habits so that we can market to different "buckets" of customer groups.

How do you make the customer want your brand as part of his/her identity? The art of advertising is getting the message through to your consumer. The communication has to be where the customer is, and the information has to be worthy of the customer's attention.

Mass Media Gets Personal

Twenty-five years ago there were three television networks, local radio only, local newspapers and many fewer magazines. There was an overall *commonality* in our media consumption and our culture as a whole. If you bought a television network commercial to run in the evening, you were reaching a third of the American population. Branding was all about getting your brand message out there to as many people as possible and repeating the message with enough consistency that eventually the message penetrated the minds of the general public. It was pretty cut and dry. You just needed money to create awareness.

Today's media is splintered into thousands of demographic/psychographic lifestyle "pieces". Kids are watching The Cartoon Channel; Teens are watching CW and Adults are watching CNN and the Discovery channel. Women are watching Lifetime and Men are watching ESPN. We can slice programming dozens of different ways from there. Not to mention the splintering of special interest magazines and the myriad of websites directed at specific lifestyle interests and habits. This relates back to the role of cloud living again.

Communication is so pervasive today; cloud living is our salvation for not getting buried in information. The goal is to surround our consumer with our message in a way that improves or enhances his/her lifestyle. This requires the direct contact of the online environment, and the exposure in the real world.

And Then COVID-19...

The value of online advertising is so much more apparent now than just five years ago. This was evident even before COVID-19 changed everything. Once the virus erupted globally, everyone conducting business of any sort had to figure out how to stay alive through the Internet. Online communication connected the consumer to the rest of the world as we were all in isolation. The long-term value of investing in the digital environment has been spotlighted even more intensely by a global community reacting together to this viral enemy. The pandemic has also heightened our collected awareness of how global our community is in so many aspects of our daily routines.

The Websites of Traditional Media

Traditional media have realized that their websites are now as valuable as their original outlets, whether it's television, radio, newspapers or magazines. The media brand attracts a mass audience and the media website can link directly to the point of purchase for an advertiser. The impact of a commercial on ABC-TV is completely different than being a click away from the point of purchase on the ABC-TV website.

Eighty percent of Millennials are not watching television on the family television screen! We can watch TV on the Internet, on our laptops, even on our phones. And we can watch our programs without commercials for a small subscription fee. Count me in! Television commercials repeated beyond anyone's tolerance to repetition do not fit into the rhythm of today's world. When the public has the opportunity to stream news and entertainment without the commercials it is the choice made. A membership fee to Amazon or Netflix or Hulu allows us to see all the television we can ever imagine without having to watch a commercial. Worth every penny.

The websites of newspaper companies are keeping the newspapers in business. The online advertising links directly to the advertiser's website. And once the consumer lands on the website, he/she is at the point of purchase. When Baby Boomers die out, the generations to follow won't discriminate as to which screen they take in information and entertainment. The websites of traditional media companies are filling up with entertainment and editorial content because of the effectiveness of their online channels for the advertisers.

The Best Messaging Traverses Channels

Today you will see TV commercials that drive the viewer to the website for multiple story endings or viewer participation. Developing content that can tie together various media channels is most ideal.

A good example of how a website can enhance traditional entertainment is the "Blair Witch Project". Back in the late 1990s there was a very successful low-budget film that developed a parallel online story, which in those days was a real creative break-through. In fact, I saw it referenced in the entertainment section of the *New York Times* recently. The "Blair Witch Project" was successful because of the integrated marketing campaign and the cult following it created through the online story. It was the web component that made money for the movie because of the uniqueness of this element at the time. It proved to be very successful financially because of the publicity from the online tie-in. The movie was actually very mediocre, but the website storyline was so unique the movie made millions of dollars.

All media companies are interactive today, which is essential in communicating with the consumer. Radio is now driving the listener to the website to *see* the things they are talking about, whether to review promotions or art that is being discussed. A number of years ago I was told that CBS Radio had more video content than any site on the web except YouTube. This is a radio-based medium with more video content than any site on the web except YouTube!

As media companies are making their own content interactive, these companies are starting to realize that the most valuable asset they can offer their advertiser is to send the viewing, reading, or listening audience to the advertiser's website where the potential consumer can interact directly with the advertisers' products.

The Big Picture: Mass Marketing for Big Budgets and Building Trust

Traditional media is generally expensive because of the mass reach. National television is the most expensive media buy but it obviously delivers the most eyeballs. It gives you the broadest exposure for creating brand awareness, but there is no direct link between who sees the commercial and the ability to react to that exposure. Unless you are a mass market brand you are paying for a lot of eyeballs that aren't your audience.

A 30-second commercial on a national television show like *Empire* is upward of $800,000. A full-page ad in the *New York Times* can be $150,000. A full page in *Vogue* is about $80,000. These all have national audiences. *Vogue* magazine doesn't have nearly the reach of the *New York Times* or *Empire*, but it has a very selective audience that advertisers are willing to pay more for. These rates are very general and approximate. They vary constantly depending on the time of year and how much advertising inventory the media companies have at any given time.

Wayfair home products are a good example of building up name recognition and trust through television and online advertising coupled together. The launch of the Wayfair brand with their TV commercials has permanently embedded their theme song in my head. As a follow-up, once I purchased products from Wayfair, I was flooded with banner ads and emails wherever I went on the web.

Bundled Multi-media Buys to Surround the Audience

The traditional media conglomerates like Murdoch, Viacom, Disney, Hearst, Conde-Nast, Bloomberg, own TV networks and many other media components, including cable, magazines, and radio. These companies now sell their media properties in "bundles". These media companies want you to buy integrated packages throughout their media landscape, offering discounted pricing in return.

In other words, if you are interested in buying a series of ads in *Bazaar* magazine and you buy Lifetime television and *O Magazine*, along with the matching websites, these are all properties of the Hearst Corporation, and they will give you a "bundled" discounted rate along with other promotional bonuses.

As long as all the components match your target audience, the bundle is a good deal because it will also enhance the brand promotion in extra ways with a multi-media buy. But if the media bundle doesn't fit your consumer it's not a bargain. Examine this opportunity carefully. When assessing these media bundles the media parent companies are willing to put together promotional packages that work more specifically for the advertiser and can be creative with an expansive reach. The media brands become *strategic partners* in communication.

Traditional media costs are negotiated. When the market is soft, or sales are really off because of the economy, the media companies are willing to negotiate the rate of the advertising buy. If you buy a series of advertising to run over a period of three to four months, you will get discounted rates. With any advertising you buy, online or offline, it is imperative to run the exposure continuously over a sustained period of time. If you can't afford to run a series of advertisements, don't spend the money because the impression will not take.

In advertising, you don't ever want to buy just one ad in any one medium. *Retention* is the name of the game for brand recognition to creep subliminally into the minds of the consumer. Think of Wayfair, State Farm or Progressive.

Localizing the Media Buy

Traditional media components bring broad audience awareness to a product. A more personalized campaign can focus on local media, even getting hyper-local by neighborhood to create awareness through special events, the local newsletter and commercials. The exposure needs to be repeated over an extended schedule of time to get the brand identity to penetrate the consumer's awareness.

This book examines how to use the technical tools and online media channels to properly communicate a brand's assets. The identity is reinforced not only by the message but also by the communication channels that are selected to convey the message. There are so many ways to get a message across and so much technology to make messaging fun and engaging. Creativity is the distinction and a highly valued commodity in the Ecommerce environment.

Online, a customer can purchase right from a link that can be inserted in any of the social channels, or in banner ads on other sites. This means the advertising is merchandising at the same time. And advertising today, as has been mentioned, is marketing driven. Today advertising encompasses promotions, phone messaging, viral messaging and dozens of other techniques that incorporate direct access to the product. Marketing today is coordinated and strategized communication using multiple touch points, all part of an integrated communications campaign which I call *surround sound messaging.*

Media departments have to be very specific about the social habits, or the psychographics of the consumer. Media buyers have to climb inside the minds of their consumers, into their lifestyles. Today's brand websites have to go way beyond their product presentation. The world of the website has to serve as a lifestyle community that you create for your customers.

Although national media buys are very costly, local media such as TV, radio, newspapers and billboards, are within reach, a little more expensive in the top five markets. Local advertising is an excellent *partner tool* for driving audiences to the Internet. This idea of personalization or localizing the message is as important to a large national corporation like JCPenney, as it is for a local Auto Dealership.

A couple of decades ago, a company like JCPenney only bought national television advertising. These companies looked at local advertising as *low class* media. Even traditional mass merchants that previously only bought national exposure now need to think about local messaging as well; tailoring the message to the neighborhood being served has even more impact. The message to the consumer should be personal, related to his or her community and daily lifestyle.

In 2006 I partnered with ABC-TV and their owned local stations to present an innovative idea using television to drive the viewer to the JCPenney website. With good music, Apple's final cut pro program, and the still visuals from the JCP catalog, we assembled 15-second commercials that would run all day in local markets with the intent of focusing on the website. Every visual is a lifestyle shot from the catalog, enhanced with music and the movement of video to give it a more sophisticated feel. The JCP website address runs across the bottom of the screen throughout the spot. Without any voice-over selling the product, we presented a graphic product shot that made the merchandise the focus, and the website address the destination.

This link https://vimeo.com/215521634 shows the three 15-second lifestyle spots created for television.

In the early 2000s when this was presented the idea that you could go right to your computer to get the goods, was a novel experience. ABC supported the idea because they knew that beyond "eyeball" measurement, they could measure the result of exactly how much merchandise would sell, since the TV spots are so product specific. This was using television to sell products from the website which is as powerful today as it was back then. The idea was too early to resonate with Penney's advertising agency.

Direct Response + the Internet

When email is supported with a direct mail piece it is more personal than local television. If an individual is going to start an Ecommerce site, my advice is always to start with a budget that affords the rental of email addresses and search word advertising and launch with a direct mail campaign. It makes an impression and it creates TRUST. This also creates a customer base for a new brand entering the market.

When sending emails, if the information is viable, or the brand is acceptable, the frequency is tolerated. This is a controversial issue but today we're used to receiving an avalanche of emails that we can eliminate or unsubscribe to if we choose. If it's a brand we like, we open the emails when we have the time or need. When you are appealing to fans of the brand you shouldn't worry about sending too many emails.

There are a lot of people who don't read their emails, but there are many more that are your audience and do read their emails every day. Email is still a very effective and personal way to communicate. If it weren't profitable, I wouldn't be getting as many emails as I get from Gilt, Nike or Amazon, every single day.

Likes on Facebook are also very valuable and can give you direct access to consumers through the Facebook feed. I had someone say to me that he doesn't interact with friends on Facebook as much as he follows businesses he likes and respects to stay up to date on those companies. That's an important comment to keep in mind.

Expanding Local Messaging

As a local merchant, chances are you can only afford to market locally. If you want to grow regionally, your website gives the public access to the merchandise no matter where they are located.

As the local advertising begins to increase your profits, you can add additional market areas to your focus with an advertising presence. This is the most effective way to start building a customer base, market-by-market. If you add a live event, maybe a Trunk Show of your merchandise, you might be able to get local publicity. Every city is looking for stories for their local 5 o'clock news.

Live Events + Email

When planning a live event, share it with the public by streaming it in real time on the website. Streaming live events gives the brand the ability to include your existing email list, while adding a new market group to your customer base. It also makes the brand more inclusive to those who only have access to the website.

When starting an Ecommerce website on a limited budget, these are the most efficient set of tools you can use for creating brand awareness. You don't need the budget of General Motors, or even Macy's.

A Note about Landing Pages

The landing page is where you are "taken" when you click on a link. It's the page one lands on when accessing a website from any link. You don't want people fumbling through the website looking for the special offer or the sign-up area for leaving an email address. They will leave the site in frustration before they find what they are looking for. This is why the landing page from an online ad is so important. Wherever you leave a link to the website it must lead to the page discussing the promotion.

Daily Communication

This is how we begin creating integrated campaigns. There are so many ways to communicate today. The best news is that all of the newer tools don't have to be expensive. Video advertising does not have to cost $200,000 a shoot. It is almost expected, or even more authentic if the video is more "real" and "engaging" looking. This is a very important element to keep in mind.

The consumer trusts an online message that isn't overly slick as more personal. The message just has to resonate with your targeted audience. Think in terms of fresh content daily. This is the rhythm of today's consumer which is very different from traditional advertising. Right now, the absolute preciseness of all brand related communication is still how traditional agencies communicate. Online communication has to grab attention through immediacy and constancy. This *allows* for a "rougher" message than the standards now accepted by this community.

Collecting and Growing an Email List

Using incentives, promotions can be designed specifically for the purpose of capturing email addresses. You can run promotions through the brand's *owned* social channels incentivizing the visitor with a discount on her next purchase, or, promote entry into a raffle. Or, you can rent email lists. Email lists can be *rented* for about 0.10–0.25 per name. The price of the lists depends on how targeted the lists are. The more specific you are in your qualifiers, the more expensive the list.

If you want to rent a list from *Oprah* magazine you need to come up with the creative content and *submit it* to *Oprah* magazine and they send it out to their list of email addresses. If you don't capture those email addresses through that promotion, you need to rent the list again. Attention needs to be placed on how to make sure the recipients respond, and emails are captured. The planning of every promotion should include email captures. Email addresses are *your direct communication link* to the consumer.

Remember, when you rent email lists you need to have the recipient go to your website and leave an email address. Then you "own" the name. You want to capture these addresses to *own* them by incentivizing the consumer. This means offering coupons, sweepstakes or invitations to special events if they register their email address.

You can run a message through the email tubes of a media company: the local business magazine, the local fashion magazine or whatever media matches the interests of your demographic audience.

If you are forming new relationships through renting email lists, by law you have to give the recipient access to OPT OUT at any time. If you say something interesting, people will read it. This is why the email subject line is so important.

A key component in the world of marketing today is collecting email addresses. This allows you to develop a *brand community,* messaging on a regular basis with this most effective personalized form of advertising. Keep it interesting and keep those emails coming.

Fashion and Music Partnerships

Fashion is like music; it's glamorous and celebrity driven which is why the web is so valuable. If you work for a fashion brand, or retail fashion brands, you have to take advantage of this. If you work for a non-fashion product it might be worth thinking about how to tie fashion/lifestyle into your communication.

Influencers and Bloggers: New Partnerships for Lifestyle *Cool*

One of the most powerful forces in the current retail industry has been the role of Influencers. Influencers have a dramatic effect on how people spend their money. Influencers have thousands and sometimes millions of people looking to them for advice in every area imaginable. Influencers, or these *style setters for the public,* are ruling the fashion industry. A whole business has cropped up around Influencers who now have agents and handsome fees for attracting the attention of huge audiences of followers hanging on every post.

Partnering with Influencers is a very effective way to get exposure for a product. There are all kinds of Influencers and just like everything else the brand touches, the Influencers have to represent the personification of the brand, the *brand style*. The choice of Influencers is vast, addressing every lifestyle need. A good partnership can create substantial recognition for your brand and expand a brand's sense of *cool*.

There are also various ways to align with these Influencers and micro-influencers: through agents, specific fees, free products, discounted products, a percentage of everything sold or a combination of the above. These individuals have such a massive following they are starting to develop their own products with major brands like Levi's and Nordstrom.

Bloggers can be speaking from inside the brand, or they can be outside Influencers who align well with the brand. Today bloggers are also powerful branding tools. Five years ago, fashion bloggers weren't a spec on the screen. Bloggers are now fashion stylists to the general public: more personalized and less idealized than a magazine's interpretation of the trends. Everyone can pick a blogger they relate to in style and they have their own fashion guru!

We exist in a world of information overload. We have to filter the information *noise* down to a manageable level. If a brand serves as a *lifestyle Sherpa* it will have open access to the consumer.

Apps

Apps allow the consumer to connect directly to the brand. Apps also present the opportunity for the brand to create a *community* among its followers with special services and direct access to all the personal information related to the brand. Apps allow a brand to create a community of brand advocates who can personally interact with the shared lifestyle of the brand followers.

And Now: Back to Surround Sound Media

As we take this very broad look at advertising and what is important about how we spend our communications budget, we start to see how the idea of becoming personal and getting inside our consumer's head can make us stand out or become *cool*. It's using modern technology thoughtfully, being careful to find out as much about our consumer as possible without invading her privacy. This helps make our communication get noticed by the customer.

This chapter has been top line information for understanding how the different media channels integrate to get a brand message through.

I am not a media maven. Media buying is another discipline with specific expertise. These last couple of chapters are designed to give you a peek behind the curtain.

When teaching my course at Parsons, my students are so proficient when developing social media marketing plans, content calendars and daily analyses for each campaign because this is their language. When a young person's adeptness with the technology is coupled with an understanding of the strategic development, the combination can grow a business substantially. Understanding the technology is only half the equation; the need for the strategic development of the messaging through the social channels is essential for effective and consistent brand building. If you understand the brand building process a young person is your best asset for execution.

Chapter 6

Strategic Partnerships for Lifestyle Marketing

Co-Branding Partnerships

It is human nature to judge others by who they associate with. That's what this chapter is about. Picking partnerships for building brand awareness is a very valuable branding tactic if the right partnerships are developed with the goal of enhancing all parties.

Strategic partners are also valuable for creating a defined lifestyle image. In order to achieve this dimensional, aspirational appeal, brands need partners. Ralph Lauren is a master at this. The Ralph Lauren website has partnered with leading art galleries around the world to enhance the RL site and give additional exposure to the gallery shows. If you are an RL customer and want to start buying art and know nothing about how to go about distinguishing good art from bad, you are going to trust that Ralph Lauren has good taste in art and the brand will educate you.

Everyone wins here: the art gallery gets mass exposure with trust authorized by Ralph Lauren, the customer gets access to knowledge that further rounds out his lifestyle choices and the Ralph Lauren brand reinforces his relationship with the customer who now visits the site more regularly.

Ralph Lauren is not going to promote anything that isn't of the highest caliber because it would question his highly protected image if he does.

We have the ability to talk to our customer even though she may be half-way around the world. The interactivity available allows us not only to track our consumer's behaviors, but also to inquire and measure her personal needs, desires and goals in life, thus filling out more of the lifestyle needs she has.

Sponsorship of and Product Placement in Entertainment

Strategic partnerships involving product placement in entertainment of all kinds, are the most successful branding tools for lifestyle marketing. To demonstrate the use of strategic partners that in the past would seem like strange bedfellows, the retailers Target and Neiman Marcus assembled a very successful promotion around the television show *Revenge*. The show aired a couple of years ago and took place in the Hamptons in New York, so everything about this ongoing evening soap opera represented a high end, luxury lifestyle. For the promotion Target created merchandise that had the same look and attitude of the luxury designer merchandise worn by the characters in the show. Neiman Marcus offered the merchandise that was actually seen in the show. This event, well publicized by Target and ABC, gave Neiman Marcus broad exposure that was unusual for a luxury market merchant. It was very well co-coordinated, certainly benefitting the Target image and increasing the ABC audience. And it was done so well that it did not reflect badly on Neiman Marcus. It was a real coup for Target to be paired with Neiman Marcus and Neiman Marcus received the exposure of a national television audience which is rare for the brand. Enhanced name recognition to a mass audience for a luxury brand, adds *mojo* or heightened credibility to the brand. This partnership featured "strange bedfellows" representing high-end/low-end, and it was a successful attempt at bringing the fantasy right to the mass-market consumer. Nothing is more powerful than being able to *buy into* the products, or the lifestyles that are seen within entertainment programming. This campaign made sure that every touch point with the consumer fit into the image of all three brands.

Magazines as Lifestyle Partners

The lifestyle magazines, online or in print, deliver specific lifestyle audiences. Does the brand Clinique for Men purchase advertising space in *Car and Driver* or *Self* or *Men's Health*, or *Vogue*? *Men's Health* may make the most sense. But maybe you're trying to get the female audience to help their men get into a skin routine, which is generally the case. Or, maybe this is too far a stretch and you need to stay focused on men who are prone to be interested in self-care.

Pooling of Resources

We must **integrate** our efforts within the workplace and throughout the daily work process to stay competitive. There has to be an environment where ideas can flow freely across departments and through all channels of distribution; across all elements involved in the process as a whole. In science, culture and more and more in education, ideas and information flow globally daily. We live in a world of integrated thinking which is always more powerful than *silo* processes. This interaction between departments is critical for today's companies.

Recently I had my students focus on the study of small lifestyle merchants that are digitally native. These merchants have just established small brick and mortar stores. These are retail concepts that are born into the future of retail. It's all about lifestyle and selling the complete image of what the brand stands for.

These merchants, especially Bonberi and Huckberry, have a very specific lifestyle defined around what they sell: specific in terms of the lifestyle they are identifying with and appealing to. These merchants opened up one location in Manhattan, a world destination in the West Village of New York, next to a few other lifestyle merchants. Bonberi and Huckberry are appealing to the same audience with different categories of merchandise. Women's Wear Daily reported recently **that, as a group,** this bundle of small merchants in the West Village are promoting and advertising in the offline world. They are joining forces to be able to communicate to the shared demographic audiences for offline advertising.

The fact that these smaller merchants are pooling their marketing dollars and cross promoting each other's merchandise is surely a new direction. Not that long ago these companies would have been considered competitors even though none of their merchandise assortments overlap. When a partnership is in harmony, the results are always more productive and diverse. In the case of Huckberry and Bonberi, and cross promoting merchandise to the same basic audience, urban, sophisticated, with an emphasis on health and well-being, this will generate considerably more traction and mobility than a single local merchant can on his/her own.

There is a very interesting chapter in Tom Friedman's book, *The World Is Flat: A Brief History of the 21st Century* (Friedman 2009). Discussing UPS and how it has integrated its services into the actual manufacturing process of a product. Back in the 1990s UPS saw the long-term impact of the Internet on the shipping industry and reconfigured its services to be able to support all the gaps the manufacturer had in its operating systems to participate in Ecommerce. UPS had to go inside a company's operating system to help the manufacturer learn how to transition from shipping in bulk to the retailers, to now being able to ship directly to the individual customer. UPS offers this assistance to any size company.

Companies were not very enthusiastic about sharing their operating systems with another company. But UPS was able to demonstrate how they could improve the product and the bottom line by using UPS as a *partner*. If they could trust UPS with this inside knowledge of their systems, they had the potential to grow their businesses exponentially.

Eventually companies did invite UPS in, and brands like Nike created products that were customized to an individual's request. The customized aspect of each product was completely built and fulfilled through the UPS warehouses and trucks. NikeID for years now has allowed the customer to design a lot of the features on many of their styles.

In today's market there are many services that will provide all of the fulfillment functions: the process of getting the product to the consumer, for a small percentage of each sale. By charging a percentage of the sales rather than a large up-front fee, the barrier of entry is considerably lower. And UPS probably makes a lot larger profit as well.

Creativity and Innovation Are Born Out of Diverse Cultures

Today everything is fused to make a better fitting part to the whole. Cultures fuse, industries fuse and creativity fuses for innovative thinking that addresses how we communicate. Urban centers like New York, Los Angeles, Chicago and Detroit have such a noticeable impact on the music and arts communities across the world because they have such a diverse population.

Every thought related to communication of the brand message has to be put on the table. Every possible idea that fits within the context of the message and the feeling of the brand experience has to be measured for relevance, budget considerations and brand enhancement value. The digital environment offers up all new ways of communicating, selling and entertaining. Corporate thinking has to adjust to the new tools and the rhythm of the online world. Experimentation is essential; trial and error are part of the process.

If Cadillac cross-promotes with Bergdorf Goodman, a unique, world-class luxury American retailer, it makes a major statement about Cadillac. Bergdorf Goodman represents the ultimate in American style. They both get what they need and both brands are enhanced by a relationship. Figuring out the creative use of linking the two brands is the challenge. Every detail needs to serve the best interests of each brand involved.

Many years ago when the American autos were just beginning to turn their businesses around with added image appeal, we assembled a video storyboard for an interactive music video. The music video tells the tale of a young woman who travels the various cultures of a disparate world quickly turning global to decide the person she wants to become. The Cadillac Escalade carries her to all of these cultures which feature the most exotic clothing from leading world-class fashion designers. This was presented in 2001 as a music video with access to the merchandise featured at a time when both the auto industry and the fashion industry were shifting focus to a global market. www.stylebranding.com/caddilac

The music video was designed to run online and position Cadillac as a global trendsetter by pairing it with the best fashion designers in the world. This demonstrates how entertainment, fashion and interactivity can impact a brand's positioning. This partnership can benefit two different categories of products, fashion and automobiles, seeking the same audience emphasizing the idea of style, luxury glamour and power.

Partnerships Are Service Tools for Your Customers

Your website should offer the dreams and desires, as well as the needs of your customers. You are creating a "community" where people with common interests or aspirations, go to spend time, chat, shop, compare notes on products, become aware, be philanthropic and relate to what your brand stands for. You as a marketer have brought all of these elements together just for your customers. You can make this happen even with one store location as a "local merchant".

Remember Citibank and how it has developed an aspirational lifestyle for its customers? It is very impressive how modern and "plugged in" the bank's lifestyle partnership choices are. By associating with the brands promoted in the Citibank's lifestyle section called *Life and Money*, Citibank establishes a lifestyle that serves young adults looking for a partner in building life's goals. Citibank takes on a whole new dimension. And the *cool* factor is established by the relevance of the references to the market Citibank is serving: young adults starting career paths for long-term planning. The references or brands Citibank promotes reflect on its ability to identify with its market.

Walmart and Moosejaw

Moosejaw is a national retailer of athletic gear. It was started by Robert Wolfe and David Jaffe from Detroit. They built Moosejaw into a national brand using good merchandise and a lot of humor and irreverence on the website. Moosejaw has developed a whole cult around the brand, and they have done a great job on their website. Moosejaw has been acquired by Walmart, which, in a sense sounds like JayZ partnering with Lawrence Welk. But in fact, it has been as successful as Lady Gaga partnering with Tony Bennett. The latest chapter of Moosejaw, an ultra-fun, hip brand, purchased by Walmart, gives you a good idea of how Walmart is staying in front of the evolution of the retail industry. It will be very interesting to see what direction this takes both brands as it is clearly a new direction for both.

Creating the right partnerships are part of the strategic development of a brand in strengthening the perception of its image. Partnering with lifestyle brands that appeal to the same audience builds a personal brand into a community. This is the goal of retailing today which has been spotlighted by pandemic times as brands learn how to strengthen their online presence. This concept creates brand loyalty: a very elusive element in the online marketplace.

Reference

Friedman, T., 2009. *The World Is Flat*, 1st ed. Bridgewater, NJ: Distributed by Paw Prints/Baker & Taylor; chap.2; pp. 141–150.

Chapter 7

Entertaining the Sale; It's All About the Story

The Value of Original Content for Online Messaging

The brand focus needs to expand from selling a product to creating an experience. There is so much content that sells and informs. Now it is necessary to develop content to *attract and engage.*

In March 2019, Tim Cook, chairman, announced Apple's new focus on content, which is the next step in this evolution now that sales for phones and watches, and hardware, are stagnant. The attention will now focus on the content that is going to fill these channels of communication. The development of original entertainment designed to exploit the assets of the Internet will become much more dimensional and *interactive* as the focus on original online content matures.

Entertaining the Sale

Online video capabilities open up a whole new arena for selling products. If we can place our products within a story context focused on the story rather than the product *sell,* it gives our products more personality. I have mentioned earlier about the art of storytelling and how powerful the role of storytelling is for engaging the consumer.

The best example of this is **product placement** promotion where advertisers pay fees to get their products featured in television shows and movies. The story is not about the product, but the products reside in the context of the story. If a movie like *James Bond* features the BMW as the car he drives, it lends tremendous *cool* to the BMW. Guys want to feel like James Bond when they drive their cars. They want to *have* the Bond car. Actually, having the product in the story content is much more powerful than a stand-alone commercial. It also elicits a deeper emotional connection with the viewer.

One of the real points of value for all of the reality shows that populate the television dial is the opportunity for advertiser support to a specialized audience. *Project Runway,* which ran for years, featured a competition among up-and-coming fashion designers. An updated version (for our streaming times) *Make the Cut* just launched a new season with Heidi Klum and my friend Tim Gunn. Obviously, this show is going to draw a lot of viewers interested in fashion and not too many engineers. If you are a brand that wants to attract people interested in fashion, like L'Oreal, this is a very good vehicle for getting the message out.

Program sponsorship creates an even stronger connection to the brand. A program that was launched on Lifetime Television, *Blush,* was to be like a *Project Runway* for makeup artists and it was produced and sponsored by Max Factor, which is owned by Procter and Gamble. So now Procter and Gamble's advertising agency is also in the television production business. *Blush* unfortunately did not last long. I guess the American public can only take so much reality. This is an example of how all the lines are now blurred between program content, sponsorship, advertising and selling.

Sponsorship of the appropriate content is going to be the future of brand messaging. The challenge is making sure the content is *relevant* and *engaging.*

This does NOT mean infomercials. There is no commercial sell in this content. The content is not about the product. It is strictly a lifestyle *positioning* statement. This lends all new value to the brand. The advertiser does not direct the content. This is about finding that fine line between selling and entertainment with the emphasis on *entertainment.* The ADmotion video walls in shopping centers in 1990 ran a continuous loop of video programming including commercials and editorial footage that was created by ADmotion (ADmotion was a StyleBranding Company). The commercials were from national advertisers like Amtrak or Sears using their television commercials. The editorial showed the products from the mall retailers draped on the top photographic models in New York. As editorial footage to accompany the commercials, we showed the products, but we didn't talk about the products.

www.stylebranding.com/admotion

Visually and emotionally, there is a big difference between showing the product and selling the product. To reach Millennials, and just about all of us these days, it is much more appealing to editorialize the product rather than sell the product. Of course, this breaks a lot of traditional rules but it's very effective especially for the voracious appetite of the social channels. Most social channels today are running images that sell and messages that inform. It is important to think about putting some cleverness or story-based content that entertains in the daily feed.

The Online Environment Demands Authenticity

We are a screen-obsessed culture: we respond more significantly to the dimension of video messaging. Today one can showcase a product using video, a phone and iMovie. By adding the appropriate music to still images on video, that movie will have 600 times the attraction of a static message.

Hands down video messaging garners significantly more responses in the social channels. Clever video can be produced quite easily with today's technology. Video can be produced from merchandise stills as long as it tells a story. And the translation of the content from catalog stills to video provides original content for in-store video displays, which will become more and more important in the store environment.

You can make sure your customer is included in the video messaging with email. You can place the video content on the Facebook page. You can use a portion of the video for online advertising which is much more effective than just a static banner ad.

Even though print has been the medium of choice for most fashion brands for as long as I've been in the business and that was before video was a medium, adapting video messaging that presents the product within an appropriate branding environment will substantially increase your social media "likes" and engagements.

Original video stories are gaining a great deal of attention especially those produced by the big fashion brands. The rhythm of the Internet is quick and fast and constant. Constant content that defines or entertains draws your community to the social channels every day.

When you are showing a product, the product is the star of the show. Take advantage of the design element, whether it's a dress or a kitchen bowl. The graphic presentation of everyday merchandise can look more enticing when the product details dominate the shot. That's what creates the seductiveness drawing the consumer into the visual. If you don't have a big budget, the product can tell the whole story. The camera has to move on the beauty or on the design element.

You can say a lot in 15 seconds and the merchandise does not have to be expensive; it only needs to look good. https://vimeo.com/474421256.

Anytime you can create a story around your product, you are enhancing the attraction of the merchandise. All the best fashion photography, especially that of the luxury brands, like Gucci, Bottega Veneta, Marc Jacobs and Dolce & Gabbana, have been telling beautiful, sometimes very erotic visual stories in print. Tom Ford head designer for Gucci at the time completely repositioned a very tired brand with his most memorable campaigns (Shaw 2019).

When partnerships occur and big brands need a unique way to create a sense of cool, the brand usually turns to music. Combining the power of music with the seduction of fashion for image and style is a winning partnership for all involved. Interactive fashion videos that combine music, fashion and access to the merchandise from the video story, can have so many applications in today's digital universe.

If the appropriate fashion brands are used to give *cool* to a lifestyle product like a car, it's a very good and productive partnership. Automobiles have very large budgets for creative ideas and style is a significant element when buying a car. Using the proper fashion brands, the car can become very seductive to the appropriate market. An upscale female consumer will relate with interest to Cadillac pairing with Virgil Abloh. The same consumer will not respond with equal curiosity if the Cadillac partner is a brand like Escada which is also a luxury brand but a much safer upscale brand. Escada does not make the same statement for Cadillac as a more cutting-edge designer who speaks loud and clear to an international audience of young wealthy fashionistas. The promotion has to be big with a lot of tentacles but again this is a very effective tool for repositioning American auto brands.

All kinds of formats will emerge going forward that have the *sell* incorporated seamlessly in the entertainment message. Using the following link, you can see how the music video concept, presented to General Motors in 2001, can influence a more youthful consumer which was the brand's goal that year. The video storyboard presents the idea of using an interactive music video telling the story of a young girl who travels the world through her fantasies to see all the things she dreams of becoming. The story features the most cutting edge, directional luxury designers in the world. She experiences the various world cultures in her Escalade which transports her from one exotic location to another. https://vimeo.com/215524608

You can use video in so many different places today that the cost to produce the content is covered through the exposure one can get in spreading the message.

You can make the programming interactive whether it's a ten-second video spot or a one-hour television special by making the products in the video for sale on the websites of the different parties participating in the promotion. This was described in the previous example using Cadillac and Bergdorf Goodman. You can run the video story on cell phones and link the video to BergdorfGoodman.com for purchase. This application is going to continue to explode over the next couple of years. It is already rampant in Asia, and we are just starting to exploit the technology. It makes so much sense. The underlining importance is to realize the value of storytelling using video and all of the unique and widespread places we can run video storytelling to sell products.

Although the above concept is an expensive one, video stories don't have to be multi-million-dollar productions. YouTube has changed all that. The requirement is that it *has to be a good story*: it has to emotionally engage the consumer. It has to grab the audience's imagination. This is what will make it viral and successful. There are very good and very bad things that capture the nation's attention through viral videos. If you're branding a product, I suggest positive exposure.

I am a great supporter of creating fantasy around the *sell*. Tell a story that transports the viewer into an aspirational world. Ralph Lauren took this idea and executed it brilliantly back in the late nineties. He created different lifestyle moods on his site allowing the viewer to engage in the lifestyle of a Southern Belle, or an Urban Sophisticate, or Western Cool. He presented the most beautiful pictures featuring all of his home and fashion merchandise to represent these various lifestyles. He added great music to enhance the mood in each lifestyle segment. This was all done with still pictures, before video streaming was dependable on the web. The consumer was emotionally immersed in the world she dreamed about... And she could have it with a click of the mouse. This always prompts me to share the image of frustrated, wealthy housewives sitting home on a dreary snowy day, clicking into this site to escape, and buying up a few things to freshen up her new wardrobe along with some new table linens. And feeling so much better!

This is the path to triggering female sales: create aspirational fantasy and let her buy into it. Everyone needs and desires some fantasy in her/his life to get through the day, and we can provide it by telling stories that include merchandising. Whether you are catering to a Goth lifestyle or a Chico's lifestyle, our *sense of fantasy* comes from the movies, television and the books we read... and the brands we shop. There is a real opportunity to be more personal with the sense of escapism.

Back in 1995 I presented and developed a proposal for Chrysler where Chrysler would sponsor a 13-week comedy series titled, *Call It Home*. It took place in New York with a young family who lived in a loft building in SoHo, and the Chrysler lived in a garage in the loft. The couple had a pronounced sense of style, as did their apartment. And the scripts were created by a well-known comedy writer, Hester Mundis, who created the perfect tone for the series and the characters; sophisticated yet self-deprecating New Yorkers who were in the know.

With every weekly episode you could purchase different items from the set design, and the set merchandise was provided by Bloomingdale's. The project was designed to give Chrysler this sense of *cool* through the pronounced style of the program environment, the characters in the show and the partnership with Bloomingdales, which has always represented an attitude of *cool*. This link will take you to a video storyboard that demonstrates how all these pieces fit together to lend Chrysler an image of *cool*: https://vimeo.com/215522456.

The public loves their television characters and celebrities. Being able to purchase anything that is a part of the characters' lifestyles can be very enticing to the audience. Back in 1995 it was too early to sell a concept like this through, but bravo Chrysler for investing in the development of this interactive television series, and having the vision to see the impact it could have on Chrysler's image when partnered with Bloomingdales and the lifestyle presented through the sitcom. The BIG bonus to Bloomingdales was having interactive television exposure in an on-going sitcom and being promoted as part of the set design on national television. Everybody wins which means the equation is a good solid business decision as well as a dynamic branding tool. The visionary marketing director of Bloomingdales at the time, Tony Spring is now Chairman and CEO of the store.

If a brand can create fantasy or aspiration it has keyed into the juice that fuels our desires. The attitude should be just beyond reach, so that the desire to achieve is possible. Think Nike.

Video for selling merchandise is a magic bullet: an emotionally charged merchandising tool. High-end brands from Burberry to Bloomingdale's are spending significant budgets on bringing video and technology into the store environment. In 1987 the first fashion on video appeared on the scene with the companies Videofashion and ADmotion's video walls. ADmotion's programming for the video walls was a media concept way before it's time. Videofashion has survived as a true representative of the power of fashion imagery on video. Clicking on the videofashion.com website will clearly demonstrate the power of fashion imagery. The impact of fashion on video couldn't be more apparent than a walk-through Hudson Yard Shopping Center in New York where fashion videos pulsate throughout the building.

Creativity Is the Magic Sauce for Brand Distinction

When my 15-year-old granddaughter was 9 she would spend time on websites where she could make movies, or where she could design clothes. But she really loved to hang out with her friends on Animal Jam where she could enter her own selected fantasy world and play with friends through these avatars that they would name and dress. Children at the age of 9 are given these tools to express their creativity. This means the role of creativity in the marketplace is going to be much more pervasive. It is critical in the world of brand distinction.

Today there are books targeting adolescents tying into a video game. The idea of learning by creating interactivity on the web tied to literary storytelling is rather common and will probably expand substantially as online learning becomes more a part of our educational culture.

Entertainment with the merchandising embedded into the content; whether for television, the Internet, movies, gaming and even print, is going to be the future of *advertising*. The product promotion is going to take place within the context of the entertainment or storytelling.

Reference

Shaw, S., 2019. Tom Ford's most risqué campaigns. [online] CR Fashion Book. Available at: <https://www.crfashionbook.com/fashion/g28797512/tom-ford-gucci-sexy-ad-campaign/?slide=4> [Accessed 20 November 2020].

Chapter 8

Merchandising an Ecommerce Website

Product merchandising is now bundled into the product promotion and the product *sell*. So far, we have focused on how to bring the consumer to the site and keep her/him engaged in the brand. But how the site is merchandised plays heavily into the customer experience.

The online space is as much about the merchandising as the marketing, and the two elements are very intricately intertwined. The eTailing Report, a company started at the dawn of Ecommerce by Lauren Freedman, helped major retailers with their online merchandising. The eTailing Report, reports on the best practices and elements that make an Ecommerce website function from a customer service perspective. These studies with mystery shoppers shopping the websites of their clients use over 100 touch points with the consumer for examining the efficiency of the site and the ease of navigation. I mention this because it demonstrates how carefully the consumer experience needs to be addressed.

One of the best ways to test the consumer experience is to have someone over 60 test the site functionality. So many sites are difficult to navigate because the minds of the young technicians who are designing and the building websites are very different from the mind of a 60-year-old when it comes to computing. And those of us in this category have a good 20+ years left of computing experience so don't count us out yet.

A good example of how the merchandising, marketing, and sales are all combined in the world of Ecommerce are the Neiman Marcus *Last Call* Lunchtime Flash Sales. Every day at lunchtime you have two hours to hunt for even better deals, and the bargains are amazing. This can only take place online, during specific hours, and it has a pronounced call to action. This is the winning combination when engaging the online audience. It becomes addictive.

Merchandising can be more creative than simply a catalog layout. With video we can do so much more towards animating the merchandise and giving the merchandise a distinctive *character*. This requires real out of the box thinking. How can I make the site fun, engaging

AND also easy to navigate? Sometimes the merchandising can be so simply enhanced with a good sense of creativity and imagination as demonstrated through this merchandising we did for the now defunct website called modestyle.com, a lifestyle website for large size women, born from a lifestyle magazine targeting that audience.

We showcased all kinds of merchandise from day clothes to expensive designer wear. We styled the merchandise without models, using the fresh ideas born of "no limits" in this new frontier of the Internet. This was back in the earliest years of this century with the technology giving us all new options. We worked with many American designers who were thrilled with this opportunity to reach the large size market with upscale merchandise through the web. We merchandised the designer collections against well-known pieces of art that connected to the merchandise through color. We took a nondescript pair of earrings and gave them character by wrapping them around a single tulip stem. The simple beauty of a tulip and its stem gave life to the very basic earrings. This was at the dawn of Ecommerce. Video was not an option yet because of the frustrating, long download time. Special effects have gotten substantially more sophisticated, but it shows you how simple it is to add dimension to the presentation. There is so much technology available to make the shopping experience more dimensional. This is the real challenge with merchandising.

Visit Your Competitors and Stay Up to Date

The best way to constantly keep your website up to date is to be aware of the sites of your competitors. By studying what other sites have incorporated into the merchandising you will stay up to date on what the web is offering. You can incorporate elements you find most effective for your brand.

I am a firm believer of having a phone number on every page of the shopping area. So often I need help and spend too much time looking for a point of contact and finally leave. I find an easily accessible phone number gives me great support when navigating a shopping site, or the social sites. Sometimes having a human walk us through the problem makes a lot more sense than the on-site instructions.

Many sites today have an iChat bubble pop-up if you linger on an image. This helpful tool appears before you have to search for it, and it's quite common on the larger retail sites. COVID-19 pushed Ecommerce into the forefront in people's daily habits. Elements, like *accessible contact*, are essential no matter the size of the company.

Remember there are no rules here and the less encumbered you are by traditional practices the more "out of the box" you become with the merchandising. Don't be afraid to experiment with how the merchandise is presented. The only rule is to make it easy for the customer to shop and clearly present the product.

Use a creative stylist and don't be afraid to show off more of the *character* of the merchandise in the social channels. Think about the art of merchandising for giving the products a personality.

Branding Partners Give Tide Detergent a Sense of Style

When merchandising to men, little *how to* pieces are so valuable. About ten years ago when creating a branding video for Target and the Young Men's department, my students very graphically showed how young guys have to go from sweats and hoodies to khakis and shirts. Since these young men, now on their own for the first time, are probably doing their own wash, the students included images like Tide detergent in the messaging, along with very cool lifestyle magazine titles as media partners. Like Target's commercials from the 1980s which changed retail advertising from product presentation to cool messaging, and presented many household products like Tide as part of Target *cool*, the students used cool images and cool lifestyle magazine partners to appeal to guys entering a new phase of their lives. The objective was to get young guys to understand the value of morphing into adult clothing. That's how you create *brand cool* or, in the case of Target, maintain *brand cool* while selling detergent!

Personal Shopper Merchandising

Stitch Fix is a website addressing customized men's and women's wardrobe needs. At stitchfix.com once you put in your measurements, your wardrobe and lifestyle needs, your shopping is done for you. The customer gets a box full of basic wardrobe pieces that all work together. And once the customer starts building a wardrobe with this *personal shopping* website, the customer is regularly sent a box of coordinating pieces of merchandise. The customer can always return what she's not interested in. Talk about *personalizing the relationship*, this is an ideal example.

Merchandising a State of Mind

Huckberry is a site with a very distinct point of view in addressing men; it consistently appeals to a man's sense of adventure and well-being. It is a site whose character or approach to lifestyle is reflected in every facet of the brand's communication. Men who appreciate that aspect in their lives will closely identify with this brand in fulfilling their goals and desires.

How Does the Customer Travel Through Your Site?

The first requirement in merchandising a website is addressing the customer looking for a specific item: how do you get the customer to that item or category as quickly and easily as possible. This customer is on a mission and you want to facilitate that as easily as possible.

Getting visitors to the site takes a lot of visibility. You want the environment to work as easily as possible. Ease of navigation is a key element in merchandising a site. Remember the landing page of a promotion when merchandising the site. If a brand runs a promotion advertised with a link from other sites, it is important to always have the landing page from the link take the visitor directly to the promotion or the merchandise presented in the promotion. Navigation is critical for maintaining customers. If it is difficult to make a purchase complete it usually results in a lost sale. Again, have different age group individuals who are not necessarily computer savvy go through the process to find out where the kinks are.

Video Brings the Merchandise to Life

Video is such a powerful tool as far as showing the merchandise on the body and how it moves, therefore you will find more and more of it in the merchandising of websites. Video is used for how-to presentations, product presentation, steaming live events, entertainment stories and all of this works. Adding lifestyle videos, cause-related video stories, testimonial videos, promotional event videos and merchandising/entertainment videos should serve every brand's websites and social channels. You can never have enough video content. Video posts get all the engagement in the social channels no matter what the brand.

The following link features a promotional video created to serve as an email reminder to Bloomingdales' consumers with a graphic presentation of the catalog merchandise. It was presented around 2006. Just like the JCPenney videos, this technique can repurpose expensive print content into video format for email and social content: https://vimeo.com/215536241.

Think about the best way possible to produce DAILY content, including video content, for the social channels. You want content that educates, informs, entertains and sells. The public now expects this constant news stream from one's favorite brands.

Website merchandising is an ideal place to put *imagination* with a capital "I" back in retail. The social channels are selling channels driving traffic directly to the web. They must be merchandised with a new point of view that takes in the full dimension of the brand characteristics.

Chapter 9

Customization

Today's technology has allowed us to get very personal with our customers. The technology also allows us to customize products to the consumer's specific needs.

Customized Products Enhance the Brand Image

Ralph Lauren capitalized on the customized element early in the game by allowing the customer to decide what color the polo horse should be along with placing the RL initials in the lower left of the shirt and adding the year to the initials. Do I really need to let everyone know how old my clothes are? Apparently yes! The ability to customize my Ralph Lauren polo shirts was too irresistible.

Customized products are a very strong draw for a brand. Shinola offers initials on all their leather goods done right in the store. One year I bought the Shinola Day Book calendars for my close friends and had them all initialed. They really loved the gift because they were personalized.

Louis Vuitton, a luxury leather goods manufacturer, created handbags that were then hand painted by Jeff Koons, a world-renowned artist featuring the works of classical artists from Monet to Da Vinci. These handbags were the *item of the moment* in the fashion magazines of Fall 2017. They are now available in the luxury after-market. But don't get excited about them unless you have upwards of $2,000 to spend. These I did not get for all my friends for the Holidays.

The online environment provides a valuable testing ground for new products that might appeal to a different audience, brands that might confuse the traditional customer in-store. This keeps the brand focus very clear while allowing the brand to test new products for market growth.

My students in the past have come up with great ideas for customized products that are all plausible. Students who studied the Bergdorf Goodman accessories group offered initialed sunglasses from Oliver's People.

One group studying Saks Fifth Avenue's contemporary department planned a promotion with Swarovski crystals as the strategic partner studding jeans from the junior department with a select number of patterns. Anytime you can create an idea on customizing a product, build a promotion around it and advertise that you are running this promotion on the website, you will generate traffic. In a world of mass consumption, consumers love individuality.

In the online world you can offer and test anything whether it's within your perceived image or out of the customary perception of the brand, like Walmart selling upscale diamonds, which they do.

All of these *cross-culture* partnerships have developed with the ease of the technology. The explosion of **masstige** as Karl Lagerfeld referred to it, has taken off in the last ten years: high-end luxury brands partnering with mass-market brands. The retailer H&M has had a series of success stories with these partnerships. The merchandise from their collaborated/limited quantity collections sell out in less than 24 hours. This limited merchandise factor creates more desire for the product.

The interesting aspect of the "masstige" concept is the story about Halston and JCPenney. Halston, who during the 1970s, was one of the most high-profile, directional American fashion designers in America. He partnered with JCPenney to take his design talent to the masses. In the 1970s this was considered heresy rather than innovative. It pretty much destroyed Halston's ready-to-wear business. Bergdorf Goodman was the first luxury retailer to drop his merchandise and it went downhill very quickly from there. It goes to show you that nothing succeeds in the wrong time frame. Halston had a great idea, just way before it became timely and acceptable.

Technology and Data Offer New Retail Concepts

As far as personalizing the brand to the consumer, all brand-related promotions are constantly personalizing the brand for the consumer. The more you can tailor the design and navigation, or the "shopping experience" to the various customer profiles, the more you are personalizing or customizing the site for the customer.

The companies that are web based native brands and work strictly from personal customer data for supplying monthly merchandise, have a solid business model for today's times. Stitch Fix has to be mentioned in this section as well. Its business model in servicing today's consumer uses tools unavailable even ten years ago. Every shopping experience is customer centric. This data driven merchandising company is excelling by creating new business models specifically for the digital environment.

When determining how to offer specialized customer service on a website, understand that most people *need* and *want* fashion/trend/

style advice as much as many of us need specific advice on electronic products. Actually, the customer is interested in any information lending additional provenance to the purchase. Offering intelligent advice is a valuable element for a trusted brand.

The Social Channels Offer Customized Service

A company needs to create awareness and trust, and the process of editing merchandise specifically for the customer's needs is always remembered favorably. Elizabeth Anthony is a women's luxury apparel retailer in Houston, Texas. Since the pandemic this local retailer fills the channels daily with information on individual products in the store describing what gives the products their provenance. The manner in which this retailer shows the merchandise is visually interesting, while the store is giving the customer details that make the merchandise that much more interesting. It's like being in the store and taking you through the selections but you can enjoy all this from the comfort of your bedroom. This is the personal *sell* that works in pandemic times. The Instagram page shopelizabethanthony has over 4,000 followers so they are doing something right.

The technology available today can offer this service to a broad audience as it functions on a very personal, one-to-one basis. A local retailer in Austin, Texas can feature a fashion stylist who might live in New York but can service those customers from anywhere online. Any fashion retailer that can create that magical experience for the shopper will have a devotee for life.

Personal Style Offers the Best Customization

Keep in mind when you are marketing fashion or lifestyle merchandise: *individual style* has been the retail mantra for at least the last 25 years. The Gap is most responsible for this message when they developed numerous campaigns around the theme "Create your Own Style". Their earliest campaigns with this theme featured a number of edgy, recognized artists from fashion, literature, dance and other arts along with new, cool emerging celebrities, all wearing Gap clothing *their individual way*. It was a great positioning campaign for a company famous for their basic merchandise.

Most consumers like to play it safe and be like their friend Susie. If you can take the consumer out of her comfort zone into a more pronounced look that reflects her personality you will have a dedicated customer. The message here is to create your own style, which is a powerful theme for personalizing the relationship between the brand and the consumer. Personal style is cool. An apparel salesperson who can help a consumer discover her/his individual sense of style has created one devoted customer.

The popularity of fashion on television has also enhanced our collected awareness of style. Style is power as it can communicate your own sense of self which causes people to take notice. Influencers, as personal stylists, have increased the interest in fashion and style exponentially. Now anyone who needs a personal stylist can find an "Influencer" she/he relates to and absorb a sense of style that feels most comfortable and expressive.

Apple has proven the value of style. Steve Jobs more than anyone I am aware of, has made this country appreciate the value of style through pronounced product design. At Apple the designers have always been as integral to the process as the engineers. It feels like Christmas anytime you unbox an Apple product. The packaging is as well designed as the products. Check out the lines at any Apple store anytime of the day or night and you will see that the *thrill* is surely worth the extra cost.

If you can show customers how to express themselves, you have empowered them. The consumer covets something she believes to be distinctive to her personally.

The challenge is to work with the online consumer so that she is comfortable and confident. Use the data you gather to best address this personal effect which will increase the image of your brand in the consumer's eye. One summer I was visiting New York and I always hit the Bergdorf sale racks in August. I was only in town for a day and had previously worked with this wonderful salesperson with great taste who handpicked through the racks for exactly what I was looking for. She was not going to be in the store the day I was in town. I told her what I was looking for and headed out to Sag Harbor for a week to be with friends. The sales rep at the store face-timed me when she was back in the store and showed me all of her selections for me. I knew what would probably work and got the package a couple of days later with exactly what I needed. That's using the technology to service a customer.

Even a small merchant can acquire daily data from Amazon regarding those who visit the site. And the social channels can give you a good idea of who is paying attention. It is essential to constantly refine the experience, keeping your brand up to date and competitive, and keeping the experience customized.

Bundled Lifestyle Websites Customize the Placement of Online Banner Ads

Previously I mentioned there are online media companies who have developed narrow and deep categories of lifestyle sites that can be used to create networks related to targeted markets. This means if you have limited advertising dollars for an online campaign you can customize the geographic/psychographic area where the banner ads will run.

Lansing Community College in Lansing, Michigan was looking to advertise online as that's where the future students are. Targeting high school students and assisted by an online media buying company, the advertising message appeared on hundreds of small sites that relate to music, entertainment, gaming or social networking within a limited geographic area encircling the greater Lansing, Michigan footprint.

Buying a regional geographic radius around a local market area, in this case, Lansing, Michigan, the school could allocate a budget of $10,000. The media buying company guarantees so many clicks with the money spent as explained previously. Even back in 2008, the school realized that advertising online was where their future students were all day long and used these tools to reach his audience instead of print ads in the local papers.

Your online audiences are much more targeted or personalized than traditional advertising. Online you can make lifestyle "buys", described above; target a specific market segment and determine the expenditure no matter how limited the budget

Programmatic Mapping for Customizing Online Ad Buying

Simply put, **programmatic advertising** is defined as targeting a specific audience related to a number of variables used to precisely define who you want to receive your message. This is how social media is bought: inserting a number of variables; lifestyle or business metrics you are targeting, and then constantly refining the effect of each variable in the message. Programmatic advertising is determined by lifestyle elements and the algorithms reflecting the combination of those lifestyle factors. Or, in the case of using this as a business tool, you define all of the business metrics you can use to describe your target audience. Sites like LinkedIn, which is a networking site for the business community, offer services to those who are part of the network, helping its members use these tools for promoting products and services. The "buys" are made electronically when you put in the qualifications you are looking for: channel of communication, age, gender, lifestyle, geographic regions, time of day, voice of message and more.

The algorithms determine who gets served the message, when he/she receives the message, and how it is received. This is computerized media buying related to social media channels. It is a key strategy for spending media dollars for the big brands.

Promotions Give You Something to Talk About

We've gotten deep enough into the story of brand cool to clearly recognize that the merchandising and the marketing are linked online. With a click of the mouse you go from the promotion to the point of purchase.

One of the most important messages of this book is the proximity of the marketing promotions to the point of purchase. Therefore, the marketing strategies have to reflect the combination of the offline elements and the online elements. It is all about thinking through what the objective is for the promotion and then fitting all of the other elements into that objective. Creativity will get you noticed every time. All of the elements we choose to focus on, whether customization or localization, or whatever theme you are addressing, those themes are built on the idea that you are consistently emotionally engaging the public in your brand.

To elaborate on the above: In planning promotional events I suggest the following basic checklist to make sure the event elements produce the results you are targeting.

1 Define your objectives as to how you want to make the brand even more dynamic.
2 Define the specific customer segments addressed through the promotion.
3 Determine the strategy on how you are going to reach those segmented groups (what marketing tools/tactics you will engage).
4 Develop a promotional calendar for the daily content in the social channels designed to promote the event.
5 Define the merchandising and measurement objectives for the campaign: what merchandise is highlighted for the promotion and what is the goal for the promotion.
6 Define basic event information for the promotion including:

    a What the promotion is; describe the promotional event in full
    b What the merchandise/marketing objective is
    c Content mapping for visualizing the media elements and messaging
    d Strategic partners whether other brands or media partners: this means **beyond** your owned social channels
    e Specific data captured
    f Wrap Up: Goals achieved, and Improvements needed

Be careful not to make the promotions so involved that there are too many undefined elements in figuring out how to make it work. Also keep in mind how necessary it is to determine exactly what data you are interested in because there is so much data available you will get lost if the specific data goals are not clear. This promotional mapping process helps you exploit the unique features offered in the digital environment.

Your objective should be to create promotions that sway the consumer to identify with the brand emotionally. The activities don't have to be related to just selling merchandise. It's about keeping the customer engaged and building a community of like-minded individuals to share information and experiences. The more creative and thoughtful you are with your ideas that enhance what the brand *stands for*, the more emotionally your audience engages in the brand.

The Distinction of a Once Great City for Brand Identity

The brand Shinola has demonstrated some of the most effective branding of our time. Shinola is a very young brand to have acquired the recognition of many luxury brands. There are a number of elements that Shinola brilliantly assembled to showcase the uniqueness in the positioning of this brand. Their advertising budgets were substantial. Shinola's presence was in all of the *right* lifestyle magazines continuously. Therefore, they created widespread recognition over the first number of years of growth. Their advertising featured endorsements from high-profile individuals like President Obama (when he was President) which also helped position the brand with that sense of desire/*cool*.

The main focus of the Shinola branding campaign was to establish the company in a city that was once recognized for its manufacturing prowess, then set up assembling product capabilities (watches) to help revive the image of Made in America. Shinola selected Detroit and used all the elements that made Detroit such a powerful world class city in the 1950s and 1960s to brand the Shinola name into the minds of the public.

Shinola borrowed from Detroit its prowess for building an internationally recognized manufacturing hub, coupled with its recognition as the town that gave birth to Motown. The power and style of automobiles coupled with the magic of the music culture reminded the world what makes Detroit *Cool*. Shinola established its brand character by emphasizing the unique character of a dynamic city.

Detroit became the headquarters for Shinola, and in return, Shinola's advertising campaign helped re-establish what makes Detroit so unique. Shinola demonstrated that with enough money and a clever point of view, traditional advertising can be very powerful in building a brand. As a native Detroiter, I am grateful for the positive awareness Shinola has created for the city, and I'm impressed whenever I see a Shinola watch on anyone, especially when I am not in Detroit.

Customized Products as Brand Distinction

Shinola as a brand offers truly customizable watches. The customer chooses the watch face from an extensive selection and then determines his/her watch band from yet another extensive selection of bands, basically making each watch a customized product. I also like to mention that even my Mother had to have a Shinola watch which she bought on the occasion of her 95th birthday. That's powerful branding considering their core audience is young men.

Good Promotions Can Lead to a Great Job

Around 2006 my Fashion Institute of Technology students had the opportunity to present their final projects analyzing the Bergdorf Goodman Ecommerce website to the President of Bergdorf Goodman. One merchandise group made an outstanding presentation; outstanding enough that the student who presented to Jim Gold, the president, was hired on the spot for their summer training program. She has just recently left Bergdorf Goodman after 13 years during which she was a successful buyer of various departments. She was also responsible for establishing the lifestyle department of unique vintage home merchandise on the seventh floor of this renowned shopping emporium, during her time there. That department is a selection of unique merchandise that only Bergdorf Goodman offers because each piece of vintage furniture is one of a kind.

When my student presented her final project to Jim Gold, the element that impressed him the most was that each promotion so precisely matched his jaded, overexposed, upscale customers. By the way this ex-student and dear friend is the one responsible for the online positioning of the Houston retailer Elizabeth Anthony mentioned in the last chapter.

For instance, the Mother's Day promotion created by the students was targeting any customer who spent over $20,000 in the jewelry department *that month*. Those who qualified entered a sweepstakes to win a trip to New York City with an invitation to the Metropolitan Museum of Art's Opening party to benefit its Costume Wing. This event at the museum is considered the most prestigious party on the fashion circuit and always features designers from around the world, along with major high-profile celebrities. Imagine the thrill for even a Bergdorf Goodman customer, to attend the equivalent of the Oscars for the fashion industry. Not only is this an event for the most high-profile taste makers worldwide, but the attire now matches the theme of the exhibit and its Fashion as Art at its best.

This story so clearly demonstrates the idea of matching an event to a very specific consumer base. Customizing products or events for specific audiences can attract new customers as well as personally service your current customers. It's not easy to come up with a special incentive for people who are able to spend $20,000 on jewelry in a month.

Brand Building Themes

As we work through these promotional themes that have been a part of the brand building process for years: strategic partnerships, customer service, customization, surround sound media communication, and cause-related marketing which we will address in Chapter 10, we can figure out how to use these themes in the Ecommerce universe. These themes give us direction in marketing properly to the customer. Most importantly they expose the character of the brand.

Now we layer our customer data, or who we are talking to, onto our strategic themes to create new and innovative concepts.

That said, there is very little that can "personalize" the brand as well as what social media allows. The interaction becomes a "conversation" instead of a "lecture". The "celebrity" factor and the *cool* factor of fashion makes the social media channels that much more interesting as the conversations unveil the personal side of the designers and the brands. Social marketing like Instagram, allows the public to feel like they are getting a look behind the curtain because of a special relationship with the brand. This also enhances the authenticity of a brand.

As a Style Maker Your Lifestyle Showcases Your Brand Identity

If you are an entrepreneur developing your own product, your lifestyle becomes part of the brand heritage. Your *style* is infused into the brand essence: the books you read, the music you listen to, the movies you like. Gwyneth Paltrow has built an empire around what she determines *cool* with her website goop.com.

Carter Young is a designer who created his first collection of unisex suits made from fine Italian fabrics while a senior at NYU. His Ecommerce website features his merchandise from a very distinct perspective. The models, the styling, the settings, and the storyline vividly describe the attitude of his clothing. His Spring 2021 collection video shows not only his merchandise but also the lifestyle that clearly represents the designer's perspective of today's street scene or his interpretation of *cool*. For a young designer trying to establish a distinct spot in the world of fashion every detail of the video talks to a very pronounced attitude which adds much more dimension to the essence of the brand. If the consumer identifies with your lifestyle tastes and desires, she will trust the products you represent. The press his Spring collection received in *Women's Wear Daily*, the *New York Times* and *Vogue Magazine* certainly reinforces the trust factor for an emerging brand.

The Power of Social Media for *Inside Access*

Therein lies the power of social media for engaging the public. The hook is the feeling of *inside access*. The challenge to fashion brands globally is to figure out how to allow the customer input on the brand while leading its devotees into newer and newer style territories. How much do you dictate and how much do you encourage input?

The very meaning of fashion is sending design in new directions. The brand has to be careful not to dilute its distinguishing characteristics while allowing customers to customize their purchases.

Capsule Collections Are Today's Norm:
The Need for *New* Never Stops

The public needs something new, something fresh, all the time. Designers have traditionally turned out massive seasonal collections that included 100+ silhouettes in some cases. The marketplace was demanding five collections a year because of the need for constant newness. This has opened up two very important trends in today's fashion markets: small capsule collections of merchandise released every month to six weeks to keep those new things coming.

Vintage Style

It is very *au courant* these days to start with sustainable products in the manufacturing. Also *au courant* in today's fashion community is the *cool* of vintage and resale shopping. Addressing the issue of overabundance, vintage and resale of designer merchandise is very popular today especially online, and these sites feature some very upscale, very high-end designer merchandise including clothing, jewelry and home furnishings. The Rockers of the 1970s as well as current celebrities have brought vintage into vogue and made it *cool*. It's all about mixing old with new, high with low, and uptown chic with downtown grunge to make it one's own. We have to adjust our thinking in a world of overabundance.

Chapter 10

Cause Related Marketing and Sustainability for Brand Distinction

Cause-related marketing is one of the finer attributes of the retail business. This is not new news but supporting a cause or a charity reflects what a brand stands for. A brand today is so much more than the product itself. When I see that a retailer is donating a certain amount of the sale to a specific cause, it makes me feel better about spending the money. When a brand exhibits a passion for making a difference using its influence with its customers, the customer feels good about incorporating that brand into one's sense of self. This is called *cause-related marketing* and is an essential tool for branding in our times.

Colin Kaepernick Takes a Knee

When Colin Kaepernick took a knee at a football game he essentially lost his career. And then Nike made him the face of their new campaign in 2018 (Creswell, Draper and Maheshwari 2018). This article from the *New York Times* also makes clear what a careful line *cause* advertising creates. An issue like Nike's backing Kaepernick and his actions, are so in tune with Nike's audience base and Nike's brand philosophy. Taking a stance made Nike extra *cool* for supporting the action and Kaepernick's message. This issue is very much aligned with the Nike brand.

These elements, the strategic partners, the customization, the support of worthy causes, all distinguish one brand from another as much as the merchandise and service do. These promotional themes should be carefully thought through as to seamlessly reflect the essence of the brand.

The Commitment Must Be Authentic

When incorporating a cause into your marketing efforts it is key that the relationship between the cause and the brand is clearly defined and that the planning of the promotion is meticulous and thoughtfully executed. The cause needs the *emotional commitment* from the brand to be significant. Incorporating the charity properly and transparently is essential.

The negative publicity of an ill-conceived fund-raising campaign can take a long time to overcome.

As mentioned throughout the book, every element added to the promotion whether graphic design or food for an event, needs to fit the image of the brand and the tastes of the audience. The ultimate objective is building the brand image and creating the desire to identify with the brand.

Attention to Detail with Cause Branding Is Essential

The complete brand strategy, including the daily social media messaging needs to be planned ahead of time making sure that all of the messaging online and offline, is consistent and focused on the brand goals.

Being creative with the cause or charity of focus can gain more attention than more traditional charities, especially if the charity specifically relates to your brand as in the Kaepernick example. Or, you may want to spotlight charities that are particularly popular with fashion brands like Project Red. The Gap has been very effective bringing awareness to Aids in Africa through Project Red, which is a number of years old now.

Fashion Targets Breast Cancer is another excellent example of the impact retail can have on supporting vital causes. This is celebrated nationally with merchants all over the country. Fashion Targets Breast Cancer was started with Ralph Lauren. It became *cool* as a fashion merchant or a fashion brand to tie into this fashion industry driven effort. With this nationwide effort and exposure, the money raised through this campaign has virtually eradicated the idea that breast cancer is a death sentence.

President Clinton wrote a very appropriate book for our times called *Giving* (Clinton 2007), which talks about the various efforts from people all over the world, and how we as individuals can contribute to helping others. It focuses on the idea that *anyone* can help another person in some way. As a brand effort, you can tie into an existing charity or create one of your own.

This trend is especially apparent in today's political climate. The George Floyd outrage and the COVID-19 pandemic have brought to the surface the voices of many companies giving support and supplies and making a difference for both of these issues. I believe that it is fundamental for brands to help our nation and our communities support those who need attention.

Young People Have the Ideas and the Accessibility

In our world of connectivity and access, young people are getting involved in noticeable ways that are creating change. Young people are making a difference in helping communities at home or halfway around the world because they inherently understand the power of the Internet. This creates a very real, broader perspective of the world as a global community. Whether helping people in their own communities, or identifying needs that exist halfway around the globe, young people are impacting change.

Micro Loans Change a Life

Micro loans are a fascinating concept. Charities online have been set up to allow you to read a profile on someone living in your neighborhood or around the world in a third world country who needs a piece of equipment or some small amount of money to create an income for his/her family. $25 can help a family to become self-sufficient. With micro loans, the individual who received the loan is required to pay it back.

In addition, there are websites like Crowdrise that work somewhat the same way where anyone can post a project or a need they have, and individuals can randomly donate to that cause.

Corporate Branding That Gives Back

City Year is a fascinating organization designed to support young children from some of the neediest inner-city neighborhoods across the country. Two City Year volunteers, fresh out of college, are assigned to each student in need of special attention for the semester. City Year is a part of AmeriCorps established by President Clinton. These students get the attention, and emotional and intellectual support they need to function at their capacity. In addition, the students are taught about philanthropy as a part of their mentoring. So even the most culturally starved students are being introduced to the value of "giving back" as part of their upbringing and education. These young graduates who serve as the student's mentors, are sponsored by various local corporations. Seeing first-hand the impact of City Year in these impoverished communities gives one hope for the future on so many levels.

Citibank and Citi Bikes is another campaign that was developed to make the community better. Citi Bikes located in heavily trafficked urban areas like New York and Chicago are a tremendous asset to these cities. And Citibank leaves a strong impression on the streets wherever they service the community with this convenient form of transportation.

I am a staunch proponent of integrating this branding element into a brand's DNA. We exist in a culture of such overabundance; this concept of cause-related branding helps bring some balance in the economic inequality. The future is about private entities addressing social problems and lending help in solving these problems whenever and however possible. I'm not talking about privatization. I'm talking about philan-thropically creating a balance.

Cause-related marketing can be promoted through many channels. Consumers don't tire of the message. Consumers respond more appreciatively if serving good while spending money.

Sustainability

Sustainability is another very hot topic today and one that Parsons School of Design is very focused on. Parsons' aggressive emphasis on sustainability related to design and apparel manufacturing is very impressive because this is where the process begins: in the fabrics that make up the apparel we all have so much of. I read recently where the fashion industry is one of the biggest contributors to waste in this country. This is a significant issue that we all need to be aware of and play our part when we can.

Sustainability is a manufacturing issue, but if the brand is focused on this as part of what it stands for, then it is essential to build this into the brand character. Everlane, an online clothing company, has done a terrific job of creating awareness of this issue with their desire to have all of their products produced from plastic waste in the near future. This focus is a vital part of Everlane's DNA. It is a noticeable element in creating distinction for their very basic but well styled merchandise. Every little bit of attention on this issue makes our environment better. Buying Everlane merchandise makes me feel better.

Going Forward Cause Marketing Will Play A Major Role in Defining a Brand

Lifestyle product and service branding is going to take a deep dive into social issues that need attention. Businesses of all sizes and disciplines will be taking on this role in society and making a commitment to making a difference.

Using the right tone for the messaging is an important ingredient in this technique. If a brand targets its audience with a cause that attracts the attention of that audience, it adds substantially to the brand character. There may be those that are turned off by the brand positioning, but they are probably not the core audience. If communicated properly, the impact of taking a stand has a meaningful effect on the audience that serves as the brand's champions, or ambassadors.

The Shinola image is a good example of a brand staking its reputation on making a difference, taking on its partnership with a very broken city at the time. One last Shinola story. When the brand set up operations in Detroit it settled in one of the poorest neighborhoods in the city, hired local employees and trained them in the art of assembling watches. They lifted the spirits of an entire city by hiring underserved individuals, and by showing off Detroit at its best. There are a lot of Detroiters walking around with Shinola watches and it is definitely a sign of *cool*.

As branding becomes more essential in the world of Ecommerce and social media, taking a stance on issues that align with your brand will have a more important role in defining your brand character.

References

Clinton, W., 2007. *Giving: how each of us can change the world*, 1st ed. New York: Alfred A. Knopf.

Creswell, J., K. Draper and S. Maheshwari, 2018. Nike nearly dropped Colin Kaepernick before embracing him. *New York Times*. September 26.

Chapter 11

Localization and Globalization

In talking about Brand *Cool* I have mentioned the importance of clearly defining your audience. Now we have to address our geographic area for doing business. I have previously mentioned the value of getting very local in the communication. We can target market segments into small local geographic groups and make a personal impact on the community with our messaging if we incorporate the local culture and touchstones. As mentioned previously, if we think locally instead of nationally even with a broad mass-market brand, our consumer can hear us more directly, or personally. With that in mind, we cannot forget that the Internet connects us with the world, and we should take advantage of that kind of reach as well.

No Limits No Boundaries But Don't Forget the Local Familiarity

When I am talking to small retailers in a resort community, I always tell them that they need to stay connected to their out-of-town clients who love all the unique little items featured in the store. If these previous customers are on your email list, with the click to the website you have an ongoing customer no matter where she lives. A few may opt out of your emails but many more will accept the communication favorably.

It stands to reason that a brand makes more of an emotional impact in a local area by embedding local culture into the messaging. Without a physical presence in the local market, a daily messaging campaign can keep the brand fresh in the minds of your customer. Diligently collecting emails, especially from tourist traffic in a resort community, builds and enhances a brand community. When using the social channels, the data tells you exactly where the respondents are from. This data helps you to reinforce certain geographic areas with the brand presence online and offline. This is an example of selling more to less which is a variation on Chris Anderson's (Anerson 2006) theme, "Selling more of less". The brand is selecting its audience and servicing this audience with all of its attention.

Glocal Thinking

Women's Wear Daily in 2019 referred to this as thinking "Glocally".

The focus becomes how to get into the community as a neighbor. Target, the retailer, is a master at supporting childhood reading, the arts, hunger and many other causes on a local level.

A website can cast a global net to engage with its luxury market consumer, far beyond the reach of a one-store location with iconic recognition like Bergdorf Goodman. The brand can make a media splash in specific markets that are dense with potential customers.

The challenge for these brands is to be visible in the real world where their customers live, even though there is no physical store nearby. Understanding how to create a presence in a location with no physical store will serve the brand well.

A robust website with an international reach can allow a brand like Bergdorf Goodman with just one store on the corner of 59th and 5th avenue in New York to continue to grow and stay competitive. It also saves the brand from drowning in real estate debt in an over-stored world as we are experiencing with so many brands in 2020. If this brand continues to focus on continually enhancing its website to create a unique experience it will survive with just one location. Whether a local one store luxury retailer unknown beyond its city limits, or a one store unit like Bergdorf Goodman famous the world over, the customer service should reach anyone who has visited your world regularly.

The Value of Pop-Up Shops

A physical presence in a community, created with a *pop-up* store can be a substantial asset for a brand trying to connect with a local community where there is no actual store presence. It serves a valuable purpose in connecting the brand on a personal level. Pop-up shops, or temporary retail locations, create anticipation, interest and traffic if promoted properly, because pop-ups by nature are temporary. If the brand is popular, this temporary location brings substantial visibility and excitement. Having a pop-up shop at high-profile festivals like Coachella, is the new *"got to be there"* marketing strategy for those targeting millennials and looking for brand cool.

Personalize the Event

When fashion designers wanted to personalize the message before the age of the Internet, they would travel to major markets and present "trunk shows" of their newest collection in person. Now we have social media so the designer can engage with his/her customers by the thousands or hundreds of thousands with a trunk full of fabulous merchandise creating multiple social media posts to last for days.

Michael Kors is a high-profile fashion designer who has taken full advantage of connecting with his clients via Twitter. In the last couple of years his brand has been mentioned as one of the leading brands in its social media reach and impact. Our culture has made fashion designers celebrities, and Kors is smart enough to spend enough time messaging through social channels to his devotees to keep them all fully engaged.

Merchandise into a Lifestyle Event

I have frequently mentioned lifestyle events featuring experts in different areas. These lifestyle events on the web may not directly relate to your merchandise but more to the lifestyle of your consumer base. You may have a live event that features a celebrity interior designer or a local interior designer. If you are an apparel store, you can feature a promotion around how to "understand your own style" on the website along with a video of his/her visit.

If appropriate, your brand can link to sites with healthy, nutritional food information because this is such an important lifestyle topic today. Any lifestyle brand can identify with personal information like this. These presentations can be offered live and streamed on the web to be part of a brand identity. Live events are designed to have an impact on a local area, but don't forget to use them as a reason to communicate through the web to a national audience interested in your brand.

Cadillac created a live event in New York specifically targeting the young luxury market consumer. Cadillac produced an upscale cooking demonstration in New York with Gwyneth Paltrow representing her website Goop. Gwyneth brought in a celebrity chef. Along with the cooking and the eating were an array of shiny, new Cadillac's on display at the event. Although this is an experience with a small very personalized audience, the event and partnership benefitted both brands. It's Gwyneth's taste level and celebrity that Cadillac is identifying with in targeting a younger audience. Good taste, good choice. And Gwyneth gets a lot of exposure from Cadillac's mailing list.

The Global Marketplace: Remember No Boundaries

Understanding the importance of communicating very personally on a local level, we cannot overlook the global exposure the Internet affords us. We should be thinking about how to start building the brand globally through the web even if we are Susie Smith selling handmade sweaters.

Luxury brands like Chanel, Armani and Gucci have opened stores throughout Asia, Russia, the United Arab Emirates, and now they are starting to go into India and China. Most of these brands are recognized worldwide and they are capitalizing on that recognition, along with the new wealth of these areas. The global spread of luxury brands is increasing at an astounding rate. Magnificent emporiums of consumerism showcasing the world's most expensive merchandise are spreading into these developing countries with amazing speed. I was called to Dubai in the United Arab Emirates in 1990 to consult on a video wall that was being installed in the *first* shopping center to be built there. Now Dubai is one of the greatest luxury markets in the world!

Some international brands partner with local retail stores in areas like India and China to learn the cultural roots of the community. This allows the brands to service these areas with more relevancy. To create recognition in a new geographic location, you must infiltrate that region with steady imagery and messaging, online and offline. Many brands believe the number of bricks and mortar stores amassed, the greater the awareness and success of the brand. Now we can do that with some ingenuity and thought just as effectively through the Internet and the aid of tools like "pop-up shops" to personalize the brand on a local level.

To create familiarity with the community a brand can create a presence in a small area and then slowly spread out as it grows its ability to accommodate the market with awareness, product and an expanding distribution base.

Test Markets That Show Interest

It is costly to operate outside of the United States, both in marketing and distribution. But you can test markets through marketing and data results, slowly expanding online access where you find customers for your brand. If you can see from Internet sales that a certain geographic region is generating sales, it becomes prudent to examine the situation and possibly produce local events in that market. The tools are there for any brand or individual to take advantage of Ecommerce effectively for growing globally. If you are in the retail business today, this should be a part of your thinking and long-term growth. As time goes on it will become easier and easier to transact globally. For a small merchant, starting to capitalize on email lists and online social marketing techniques is key to future growth.

Don't Overlook an Interested Audience

I took a Sabbatical a couple of years ago in 2012 settling in a small beach community on the shore of Lake Michigan. While there, I was trying to show this community of local merchants in a resort area that they can stay connected to their customers who come from all over the world to visit the Eastern shore of Lake Michigan. This can be done with constant communication through the website.

Many of the products in resort communities are local and indigenous to the area. If a customer wanders into your store and she happens to be from Wales and she just adores all those little things she was able to find for her grandchildren, she feels connected to you all year round through your emails. And, during the holiday shopping season if she really wants more of your unique items, you're right there in her daily thoughts with lots of new ideas for those grandchildren of hers.

In today's world, if you have a customer's email address, you can stay connected no matter where she lives. If the customer likes your products in person, she will continue to shop with you long distance if the service is good and the technology is easy to navigate. COVID-19 helped everyone adapt to Ecommerce shopping. Suffering a global pandemic together also hastened the idea of our global community.

This "glocal" trend will continue to be more and more prevalent in the next couple of years. If you have a unique mix of products people will search for you and be interested in your product no matter where you are located. It's all about keyword search and advertising.

It Takes a Global Village to Build a Sweater

Almost 15 years ago I worked with Fashion Institute of Technology putting together two weeks of lectures for a Global Fashion Management program that involved students from Paris, New York and Hong Kong. Paris is the center for design, Hong Kong is the center for manufacturing and New York is the center for marketing and communication of a Fashion Brand. The objective was to show this international group of Business students the full process of the fashion business

My job was to put together presentations that focused on the advertising or marketing of Fashion. One of the presentations we scheduled for the group was with the president of polo.com. Ralph Lauren was one of the first and one of the best at putting together a lifestyle website as I have mentioned throughout the book. But the students were quite surprised that polo.com wasn't set up for Ecommerce in Europe at the time. Ralph Lauren is certainly a high-profile brand internationally, and the technology was available. Since then RL has expanded the retail business internationally with store fronts in Europe and staging a huge event in Paris to brand his presence throughout the continent.

RL has been slow at expanding internationally into the markets where the brand is known. The facilities were available even back then because companies like UPS offered a complete package of services for assisting companies in getting the product from the warehouse in the States to wherever in the world it needs to go. The brand is feeling the pain of not aggressively getting into these new areas of growth. Today global visibility and interaction is a must for brands like Ralph Lauren as a way to keep profits growing.

Breaking Down the Barriers of Entry for Reaching the Global Market

Overseas delivery systems like UPS and FEDEX have sophisticated services in place for setting up global distribution for an Ecommerce retailer (UPS.com).

UPS has built a very modern and accommodating business model for supplying back-end Ecommerce functionality. The UPS systems work as efficiently for a local mom and pop operation as they do for a global brand like Ralph Lauren. UPS goes into the company to assess how the shipping department is set up and how to improve it. In some cases, the final steps of customization or product development are actually performed by UPS before the product is shipped.

If Susie Smith is selling custom made cashmeres online and wants to ship overseas, UPS will package the product, handle all shipping information, generate the communication emails to the consumer on tracking the package and handle tariffs issues. UPS charges Susie a small fee up front and a small percentage of each item it ships.

The fee to UPS is based on the sales that are generated. And UPS makes money when Susie makes money. UPS is a company that in the last 25 years has completely changed its business model to fit the changing needs of the economy.

And then there is Shopify, mentioned previously, a website that puts the entire process together for anyone who has a product or a service for the marketplace. The site readies thousands of entrepreneurs offering all the services needed for building their individual empires from the ground up; professional and built to last.

Accommodating Local Customs

Whether you are going into Arkansas or India the first issue is understanding the culture you are interested in interacting with. What are the local customs and traditions, and how does your product interact with those customs?

You should never go into a market without addressing the needs and cultural specifications for that market. Does this community really need the product? Fur coats are not going to sell in Maui and McDonald's hamburgers are not going to sell in India. In the case of McDonald's, they created different meat-less products in India because of the sacred-ness of the cow in that culture.

The more you take on the native culture, the more accepting the culture becomes to a foreign brand. This is true whether you are going state-to-state, or country-to-country. As our cultures are becoming so integrated and cross-pollinated, we need to adapt our products for the global needs and differences. American designers who are selling their garments in the mid-east and India adapt the collections to their customer's needs while maintaining the look that made the garment so desirable in the first place.

Ah... but the Lure of American Brands

Yet we also have to acknowledge the popularity of American brands worldwide; foreigners are fascinated with American products and can't get enough. The dollar is still cheap, and we have an alluring pop culture. Many foreigners want American products just because of the brand name: a Marc Jacobs purse for instance. You have to be aware of the culture you are about to market to and finely tune the product to be acceptable in that culture.

Many of the high-end designers specialize in small sizes because their clothes look best in small sizes. This specifically caters to the Asian market. Many designers have incorporated a lot of bright color in their designs influenced by their Indian customers. When American auto companies sell their brands overseas, they create smaller models to accommodate the crude and narrow roadways, or the over-populated areas like Tokyo. You will notice that the United States has the *biggest* cars you will see because BIG sells here, they make more money from big cars, and our road systems can accommodate these vehicles.

Companies that have distributed globally for some time now are very adept at assimilating the product into the culture: Proctor & Gamble for instance; toothpaste, Tide, etc. expanded globally and in some instances translated the name to the local language. In some cases, Procter & Gamble has changed the name altogether.

Customizing the products for distribution or customizing the marketing to suit specific local customs is something that needs to be thoroughly researched and strategized before initiating any expansion activity.

We are all part of a global economy and going forward that is going to be where we grow the fastest and most extensively. If you are placing a product in today's marketplace, you need to be aware of the globali-zation of commerce even if you are Suzie Smith. The more effective we are at understanding local customs the more our product relates to our growing market of consumers.

References

Anderson, C., 2006. *The long tail*, 1st ed. New York: Hyperion.

UPS.com. 2020. *Worldship Support | UPS Services - United States*. Available at: <http://www.ups.com/content/us/en/resources/techsupport/worldship/index.html>

Chapter 12

Imagine the Possibilities; the Role of Virtual Reality in the Future of Retail

From my perspective, having seen the profound significance of Ecommerce back in the mid-1990s, the retail industry resists change as much as the next guy. Change is very difficult and as mentioned earlier, for the retail industry over the last 25 years, Ecommerce has been the equivalent to learning an obscure foreign language.

But, all of a sudden, the world is learning very personally that even though we are quarantined at home, anyone anywhere in the world can access just about anything with the right technology. As far as I can see, this trumps all other selling venues: one central location that displays all your products which anyone can come to from anywhere.

Potential customers are coming to you from all over the world. You don't need a store or many stores; you don't need the expense of printing and sending catalogs. All you need is a good idea, email addresses, functioning links and social media accounts. A little budget for online media buying takes you a long way. For $10 you can generally land 500–1,000 impressions.

Technology Will Create Our Greatest Fantasies Online and In-store

I imagine that very soon major retail brands are going to create truly unique visual and emotional experiences through the brand's website. The Flagship location should be the website; flagship being the location that best shows off the full array of the brand's products and clearly personifies the brand's *state of mind.*

Ever since the late 1950s the sign of retail success has been to have as many brick and mortar locations as possible. This growth was fueled by the shopping center industry which was populating the country and the rest of the civilized world with state-of-the-art retail emporiums.

The more popular the brand became, the more the need to spread geographically through local malls to give more access to the product. Building more and more stores demonstrated more and more popularity and brand success. Building brand recognition in new markets was easily facilitated with local print advertising.

Now there is access to shopping 24 hours a day, from retailers around the world all from my kitchen table. During the early stages of the pandemic of 2020 Ecommerce was pretty much the only game in town. Now, and rightly so, everyone who offers any product or service is scrambling to figure out how to dress up the website to be able to interact with customers. It is my opinion that a budget allocated to build and maintain a new store location would be substantially more productive if fed into the online presence of the Brand.

Disruptors That Create Change and Innovative Thinking

Too Many Stores

This brings us to the next major disruption in the industry: the obsolescence of such an overabundance of retail stores. People aren't going to the stores as much as they used to. The ease of shopping from home, having access to anything one's heart desires, the ability to compare prices and in many cases the offer of free shipping are much too irresistible to deny. And vintage everything is more popular now than ever before.

I knew shopping habits have significantly changed when I heard a friend of mine, a consummate shopper living on Fifth Avenue in New York, tell me that she "NEVER goes into stores anymore, NEVER". I'm sure her "NEVER" is a little exaggerated because the thrill of store shopping never *completely* dies.

Stores are not going away. We all have the basic desire to socialize. But the retail environment is going to change very dramatically over the next five years. The in-store space is going to be much more interactive because we are used to and conditioned to multi-levels of stimulation. The stores need to offer something beyond the presentation and purchase of merchandise.

Reimagining the Mall to Address Modern Lifestyles

The malls will offer more experiential environments where mountain climbing simulation might be available, or water parks along with skating rinks. Restaurants and artful food presentations are going to be more prevalent in malls. In-store shopping experiences are going to be very different than they are today. WeWork, a common workspace for today's independent worker, is replacing the department store anchors in malls. Rent the Runway has space within WeWork, another convenience that makes the mall vital to the lifestyle of young adults today. Rent the Runway is an online retailer offering the ability to *rent* designer merchandise. Even Amazon is opening stores in malls these days. The malls are going through a major upheaval and the best are remerchandising to address our new living patterns.

Social Media Is the Magic Bullet That Changed Everything

This leads to the biggest disruptor, social media. If one sets up a Facebook page, twitter, Instagram and YouTube accounts, one can sell products and allow customers to personally engage in the brand experience. Allowing a consumer to comment and input her feelings about the brand allows her to feel a part of the brand community. It is empowering for the customer, in addition to presenting brand transparency.

The real magic bullet is the multitude of functions social media provides the retailer for marketing the brand attributes. Social media very effectively tells the brand story, builds brand awareness, sells the product to the consumer and allows the customer to endorse and sell the product to friends.

Hands down social media communication should always win when allocating budgeting dollars. From Influencers who are personal shoppers to the world, to AdWord advertising, and social media marketing tactics, these are all tools for building brand *cool*.

Social media, for the most part, is the language of Generation Z and Millennials. It's a brand-new language brought into the world by "twenty something's", and powerful enough to up-end billions of marketing dollars worldwide.

Social media marketing tactics are now a fundamental part of every brand's marketing plan. Thanks to the technology, there is so much information allowing today's marketers access to the precise needs and desires of a brand's consumer community. Harnessing this opportunity properly is the golden egg in today's marketing landscape.

The Science of Online Marketing

In the early days of AdWord advertising a friend Steve Goldberg who was a specialist in this newly forming industry, would guest lecture to my class always stating: "Understanding the system is like coining money". You are able to articulate so many variables in selecting your online audience, learn in real time what variables are working and have the ability to reposition everything accordingly. This literally guarantees increased exposure and sales. Your online audience is so vast, the more precisely you can pinpoint exactly who you want to talk to in this far reaching universe, the more successful your results.

Online Media Buying Simulations Are a Great Learning Tool

My Parson's students had access to Stukent which offers educational simulation materials that actually allow the students to see how and why the social media buying tactics work. As mentioned earlier in the book, there are online services that offer these simulation services to the public, like Google or Hootsuite. In simulating the use of these services it becomes quite clear how valuable this tool is in the branding process.

Today Everyone Has Access to Style

Before the Internet, if you were a Sears or Walmart shopper, it would take a year for the major fashion trends to filter down to the mass market. Now you can be in Fargo, North Dakota and if so inclined, with a good connection you can find out what's *cool* as soon as it appears in the marketplace and...you can purchase it!

The Power of Influencers

Along with instant access, we live in a world populated by *Influencers* who are there to help us develop our own sense of style. If you were not raised with a complete passion for the fashion industry and you want to be more pronounced with your sense of style, you can go online and find an Influencer or *style setter*, who you relate to. This helps you develop your own take on how to face the world.

There are all kinds of Influencers: celebrities like Gwyneth Paltrow, fashion stylists and anyone who is confident enough and aggressive enough to garner a following dependent on their daily advice related to what's *cool*.

When an Influencer has hundreds of thousands of followers, all of a sudden his/her opinion becomes very important to the retail industry. For a brand, Influencers can be very powerful for promoting merchandise; therefore, they need to be rewarded accordingly. It's a new industry and the rules are wide open. The issue is to work out a win/win situation so that the Influencer benefits from the sales he/she generates. Finding the right Influencers and creating a mutually beneficial relationship with the Influencer is what you need to keep in mind when engaging in partnering with these high-profile individuals.

Taking it a step further, understanding how these Influencers communicate is key as well.

An Influencer can be very high profile but not prolific with posting. This is not as valuable as an Influencer who is constantly "pumping" out information. Connectivity is key with Influencers. That's their value. If they are connected to other Influencers they bring more to the table because they act as a "hub" of information that is then traded with other Influencers. Communication and content are always the driving factor. Just like every other element related to the brand communication, the Influencer has to reflect the essence of the brand

New Communication Content Is Necessary for the Web

These valuable tools have been laid at our feet but the challenge is content. The Internet is a voracious beast and today's consumer expects fresh content daily. Content is the trigger for engagement, which means the content has to grab attention and sell. At the point of engagement you can register a response. This gives you information on customer response in real time, all the time.

When one is assessing the planning and analysis of the brand communication, it is essential to focus on what encourages awareness and engagement: what *excites* the customer. Engagement is as important as a sale. Are there increases in mention of the brand? Is there an increase in traffic to the site, or the social channels? Is there an increase in page views and is there an increase in engagement? Keep posting and testing and you will see what excites the audience in real time. Building a community of customers who respect the totality of what the "brand stands for" is the goal.

Testimonials

Testimonials become a valuable tool in this new retail landscape. Testimonials support the brand transparency and authenticity. The public trusts the opinions of others. This is a very persuasive brand qualifier.

Merchandising the Experience

It's important to remember most individuals under 45 today are wired to think technology first in solving problems and shopping. Thinking about how you are going to create engagement is as essential as the purchase. This will be more and more important as Generation Z, and those generations following, move into the consumer market more dramatically and the Baby Boomer generation is of another time.

Social media content can maintain this engagement if it serves the customer's needs and desires in some form. As we start to look at merchandising more experientially, all kinds of opportunities can open up as to how we communicate the brand story. This is the thinking you should be tapping into. The more imaginative your thinking, the more unique the experience.

A simple example: In support of attracting active, adventurous, professional men, Shinola has interpreted this idea in a unique promotion sending photographers to places like Peru to capture the exotic landscape and tell the story of the travel experience. Shinola sends the photographer to the location with a Shinola satchel and asks the photographer to report on the area through his point of view. This campaign speaks to the core target audience of the brand, and taps into an interesting lifestyle feature appealing to that audience making the brand *feel* exciting and adventurous as it takes its customers to exotic places.

The more variety and original content you put into the mix, the more responsive and engaged your audience becomes. The need for content is so demanding that you can have a variety of content formats telling the brand story whether it's Influencers, testimonials, photographs from shoots or original content. All of it can be used harmoniously to create the brand experience.

The need for content is going to increase as time goes on, and new viable merchandising concepts will flourish. Content creation is going to be big business over the next couple of years as brands continue to develop and exploit these digital tools.

My personal focus has always been on creating unique content for brand exposure. Having produced fashion shows of all sizes, I am always focused on wrapping the "sell" in entertainment.

One of the change elements in this book is to realize how social media communication needs to be taken seriously and planned strategically in the overall branding campaign. Once you address these variables seriously; mapping out the daily content and media buys; implementing the plans and then carefully assessing the results, you have control over the productivity of the campaign, the movement of your products and the brand perception.

Optimization Makes Sure the Message Gets Through

When these issues are routinely addressed, you are pretty much guaranteed success. Since everything is measured in real time, the ability to *optimize* the campaign week to week makes it even more efficient and productive. With real time information on how the campaign elements are drawing interest, you can watch the campaign meet the goals needed for success. The metrics of engagement can be gauged through the following elements:

- Number of clicks on the content, and how many times it has been shared

- Increase in positive attitude by the consumer base
- An increase in testimonials and product ratings (bad ratings help pinpoint a problem and communicate a solution quickly)

All forms of media; earned, owned and bought, can be measured, and, using these metrics keeps us ahead of the curve with our brand communication.

This analysis of social media marketing has been designed to demonstrate how Ecommerce has invaded the retail industry, and why it is important to creatively adapt traditional branding strategies to social media communication and use the tools the technology affords.

Where Are We Going?

In the 1980s and 1990s, stores began to multiply the number of brick and mortar units, as shopping centers became the center of our communities. As most retailers were expanding their physical presence across the country, Amazon was completely focused on how to create *comfort* and *trust* in this new retail universe. As Amazon continued to grow into the colossal brand it is today, the focus has always been on customer experience rather than the bottom line. This is a very good lesson to take to heart. If the focus of the brand is on creating an experience that enhances the interaction the customer expects, the brand will have a reputation that satisfies personal and emotional needs. The **customer experience** has always been the primary focus of successful brands.

I started this book with the story of how I realized the power and convenience of the Internet in the mid-1990s, at Christmas time. Shopping for my Granddaughter I realized I didn't have to go to the mall, wait in long lines, carry packages around and then have to wrap and send the gifts out of town. I could go to Toys.com, pick out the appropriate gifts with help from the site and ship the packages right to my loved ones. It couldn't have been clearer to me, that kind of convenience was not going to go away. Although toys.com is no longer in business, the Internet is the basis of our economy.

All these years later retail brands are surely convinced of the power of the Internet. Most major retailers consider the Internet an integral part of the brand experience and offer a fairly comprehensive array of merchandise on their sites. Retailers are also learning to use their social channels to help spread the point of sale for the brand. But we haven't begun to exploit the imaginative environments we need to create for expressing brand distinction and fantasy. Retail emporiums have always been about forgetting your troubles and surrounding yourself with beautiful things that make you happy.

And the Future...

As we continue to build our websites into our brand alter egos, the boundaries of brand expression need to expand extensively. Virtual Reality is going to play a significant role in the in-store and online experiences. It may be worth going to the Mall if Gucci's new season's clothes are presented at the Roman Colosseum through a Virtual Reality experience. I also believe that brand websites will become virtual trips into the fantasies we most desire.

I speak of the Internet as the great frontier of retail because it has a long way to go in exploiting the potential. Just as so many new retail concepts have come from the Internet, like Birchbox, Stitch Fix or Rent the Runway, the appearance of more aspirational or fantasy environments will start to appear. The excitement in retail has always come from imagination, creativity and the exploitation of desire.

Just as Marvin Traub at Bloomingdale's, Stanley Marcus at Neiman Marcus and Phil Knight at Nike, took us out of the mundane of daily existence, the merchants of tomorrow will be able to take us to places presently unknown. We need to reward creative thinking and taking risks. We all need the input of young minds for maneuvering through the social channels. But also needed with all this creativity is the understanding of strategic thinking.

In taking you inside the world of Internet marketing and Ecommerce I hope I have given you the tools to think creatively and approach your web experience as a unique statement of purpose. How do you make your customer experience distinctive and exceptional? Whether you are Susie Smith with the hand-made sweaters, or Amazon, this book will guide you to success.

Let me know how it goes.

joanie@stylebranding.com

Index

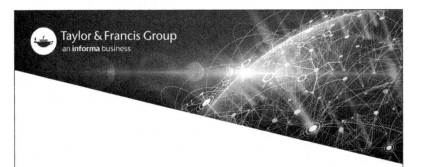

Printed in the United States
by Baker & Taylor Publisher Services